# A STUDENT GUIDE TO

# Writing a Research Paper

## A STEP-BY-STEP APPROACH

### PHYLLIS GOLDENBERG

**Sadlier-Oxford**
A Division of William H. Sadlier, Inc.
New York, NY 10005-1002

## Acknowledgments

The publisher wishes to thank students Andrea Wang and Leslie Porter for permission to use their research papers in this book and the following individuals for their contributions as reviewers and consultants:

| Curriculum Reviewers | Student Reviewers |
|---|---|
| Frederick J. Panzer | Michael Dinger |
| Christopher Columbus High School | Garden City, New York |
| Miami, Florida | |
| | |
| Patricia Stack | Elizabeth O'Donnell |
| South Park School District | Yardley, Pennsylvania |
| Library, Pennsylvania | |
| | |
| Paul David Rivadue | Cynthia Dinger |
| Garden City High School | Larchmont, New York |
| Garden City, New York | |
| | |
| Thomas Pasko | |
| Saint Ignatius High School | |
| Cleveland, Ohio | |

Cartoon Research by Photosearch, Inc.
Design and Composition, Creatives, Inc.

Printed in the United States of America
ISBN: 0-8215-0760-5
56789/04 03 02 01 00

# Ten Steps to a Successful Research Paper

Sadlier-Oxford's *A Student Guide to Writing a Research Paper* presents a unique, step-by-step approach that helps focus students on the tasks of moving through the research-paper process in an innovative and efficient way—by encouraging them to complete their own research papers as they complete this book.

At each step students are introduced to a key element of the process, then given exercises to help them practice and master that element, and finally prompted to apply or incorporate it in their own research papers.

In content and method *A Student Guide to Writing a Research Paper* is designed to be equally useful to those students who are writing a research paper for the first time and those who have many such papers behind them. For first-time writers this book provides a clearly organized plan—from choosing the topic to submitting the finished paper—as well as a wealth of practical advice. For more experienced writers the book will prove a handy review and reference manual, complete with reminders, cautions, and hints to help assure better-planned and better-written papers.

# Special Features

- **Computer Connections**   Tips for students who use computers and word-processing programs for their research-paper projects

- **Hints**   Useful advice meant to facilitate the research-paper process

- **Checklist Reviews**   End-of-chapter recaps

- **Cartoons**   Chapter openers focusing on the lighter side of the writing process

- **Timetables**   Suggested schedules for completing the project

- **Appendices**   Three supplements providing information on reference materials, alternate formats and styles, topic ideas across the curriculum

# ▶ Contents

# Preface

By the time you finish this book, you will have transformed blank sheets of paper into a coherent, fact-filled, smooth-sounding research paper that you can be proud of. In the process, you will become a local expert on the topic you have chosen to write about. You will probably end up knowing a great deal more about your topic than any of your classmates, friends, or family. What you find out about your topic will stay with you a long, long time.

That's the *content*—the information you discover.

Research also involves a *process*—how you go about unearthing information.

Think of this book as tool kit and map combined in one handy package. It will give you all of the tools—the essential skills—you need in order to plan and complete your research paper, and it will guide you—that's the map part—every step of the way. Literally, you will complete ten steps in the research process.

As you research and write, you will be working some of the time with a partner or with a small group. You and your classmates will advise and support each other as you compare notes on your progress and discoveries and comment on each other's work.

If this book belongs to you, keep it. No matter how many research papers you are asked to write in the future, the steps of researching and writing will be the same. The content of your future papers will change, but the process will remain the same.

Are you feeling curious? nervous? impatient to begin? You're only ten steps away from your finished research paper, so step right up for Step 1—and have a great time!

Phyllis Goldenberg

# Choose a Topic

PEANUTS reprinted with permission of UFS, Inc.

**S**o you have to write a research paper. You have just been handed one of the most interesting—and challenging—writing assignments of your school career. To complete the assignment on time you will need to begin promptly and keep plugging away until you have finished. (On page 137 of this book you will find model timetables that may help you plan your own project.) So let's get started! The first thing you will need to do is decide what you are going to write about.

## Before You Begin

### Make sure you understand your assignment.

A research paper is a long, formal essay or report that presents information from a number of sources. You will need to know exactly when your paper is due, how long it is supposed to be, and what type of research paper you are expected to write.

**Length.** Your teacher may specify a paper ranging in length between 1,000 and 2,000 words (sometimes more). You can estimate 250 typed words to a double-spaced page to determine the number of pages of text you will need. Or your teacher may assign a specific number of pages—five to seven double-spaced pages of text, for example. Listen carefully to the assignment, and follow the

specifications (for length, topic, type of paper, style of documentation) exactly.

Keep in mind that whenever you write a report, explain an idea, or write a memo or proposal, your writing is **expository** in nature: your purpose is to inform or explain. You are not telling a story (that is **narrative** writing) or describing something or trying to convince someone to do something. In expository writing, your purpose is chiefly to convey information to your reader.

**Audience.** Usually your teacher and your classmates are your audience, but sometimes a research paper can be shared with others who are interested in your topic. For instance, if you have written a paper about a strong-mayor vs. city-commission form of government, you might read and discuss your paper with a government class or send it to your local governing body. If you have written about recent legislation protecting manatees, you might share your findings with the school's science club or a local environmental organization.

**Types of research papers.** Research papers, which are sometimes called term papers or library reports, can be classified as either **informational** or **analytical**.

An informational paper summarizes factual information from a variety of sources. The writer's task in such a paper is to focus the topic, find the information, and produce an organized and coherent paper.

An analytical, or evaluative, paper goes one step further. In this kind of paper, the writer analyzes the information and presents his or her conclusions. An analytical research paper displays some of the elements of persuasive writing since it states the writer's opinion and supports it with detailed evidence.

Make sure you understand at the outset whether your teacher wants an informational research paper or an analytical paper. Here are some examples of topics for each type:

▶ **INFORMATIONAL** Recent developments in electric-powered cars

▶ **ANALYTICAL** Three reasons why electric-powered cars have not gained wide acceptance

▶ **INFORMATIONAL** New-car prices cause boom in sales of used cars

▶ **ANALYTICAL** How to be an educated used-car buyer—what to look for and avoid

## Choosing a Topic

**If a specific topic is assigned.** Be grateful and get going. Rarely, however, does a teacher require everyone to write on the same topic. When more than one person is working on a specific topic, source materials become hard to find since several people are competing for them. Also, most teachers prefer reading about a variety of topics instead of the same one over and over.

**If the general subject is assigned but not the specific topic**. If your teacher assigns a general subject and lets you limit it to a workable topic, part of your job is already done. Limiting is easy, once you get started. (See page 11 for examples of and suggestions for cluster diagrams.)

**If it's totally up to you.** This is the usual scenario: Your teacher lets you decide what to write about and simply requires that he or she approve your topic once you have chosen it. It is important to settle as soon as possible on a workable topic—you have a lot of work to do once you have chosen a topic and had it approved. (See Appendix C for suggestions for topics that might interest you.)

**HINT**

You don't have to find "The Perfect Topic" (it probably doesn't exist anyway). You just have to find a *workable* one.

**Choose a workable topic that meets all of the following requirements.**

**1. You can find enough material on the topic.** Usually, a research assignment calls for at least five diverse sources, some print and some nonprint. Sometimes, for instance, you will be expected to conduct an interview to serve as one of your sources. Avoid choosing a topic that is too recent or too technical—you will have trouble locating information. Once you have chosen a topic, do a quick check in your library or media center (see Step 2) to verify that there are available five or more sources on your topic.

**2. The topic interests you, and you think you can make it interest your audience.** An ideal topic tickles your curiosity. You may know something about it already, but you would like to know more. After all, you are going to spend many weeks immersed in the topic. Ask yourself if you would like to become the class "expert" on this topic.

Take an interest inventory. Start by taking stock of the things you are interested in. List as many as possible. For example, you might include your hobbies; your ambitions and goals; careers you are interested in; places you would like to visit; things you are curious about (ideas; how something works and why); the biggest problems in your community, country, world; things you would buy if you had all the money you wanted; ten famous people you admire—and a word or two about why you admire each.

Look for topic ideas. Explore as many sources as possible for possible research paper topics: Browse through newspapers and magazines. Talk to relatives, friends, experts. Interview someone. Listen to radio talk shows, National Public Radio, news shows. Watch TV documentaries and the evening news. Browse through the documentary section of a video store. Browse through a library or bookstore. Check out electronic magazines and newspapers on a computer. Flip through an encyclopedia.

**EXERCISE 1**

## Brainstorm

Alone or with a partner or small group, brainstorm topics that interest you. Make a list of ideas and suggestions, including those that you gathered in your "interest inventory." Then review the list and choose the three topics you would most like to write about.

_____

_____

_____

_____

_____

_____

_____

_____

_____

_____

_____

**3. The topic is objective, not subjective.** An objective topic is factual, not personal. Generally, in a research paper you are not writing about your opinions, your experiences, your friends and relatives, your feelings and ideas. These are subjective topics. Here are some examples of each type:

▶ **OBJECTIVE** Evidence for and against side airbags in cars

▶ **SUBJECTIVE** My uncle's car accident

▶ **OBJECTIVE** Signing up the voters: techniques for registering new voters

▶ **SUBJECTIVE** What happened when I tried to register to vote

**4. The topic is limited enough to be covered adequately in the space available to you.** You will need to focus your topic until it's just the right size. You can't, for example, write a research paper on the history of China; you would need a whole book—or several—to cover such a broad subject. Limit, or narrow, your topic to one that can be covered thoroughly in the space you have available. On pages 10–15, you will

▬▬▬▬▬▬ **HINT** ▬▬▬▬▬▬

If you can find several books devoted to your topic, the topic is too broad and general and needs to be limited further. For example, if you choose to write about American Indian mythology and find six books on that subject listed in your library's catalog, your topic needs to be narrowed further.

learn some techniques for limiting a general subject. But do not choose a topic so narrow that you can cover it completely in a paragraph or two.

▶ **TOO GENERAL** Ants

▶ **STILL TOO GENERAL** Fire ants

▶ **STILL TOO GENERAL** The evolution of fire ants

▶ **JUST RIGHT** The invasion of fire ants in the United States

▶ **TOO LIMITED** What to do if you are stung by a fire ant

▶ **TOO LIMITED** What a fire ant looks like

## Computer Connection

Use a search engine to browse through the listings on a general topic. (A search engine is a tool that enables you to target and access information on the Internet.) If you enter the word *karate*, for instance, you will come up with hundreds of listings, and they will all be more limited in some way than the general word *karate*. Maybe you will get some ideas of more limited topics.

## Clustering

A **cluster diagram** is a doodle with a purpose, a graphic device for limiting a general subject to workable topics. Start by writing the big idea—a broad, general subject—in the middle of a piece of paper, and circle it. Then break the big idea into its parts or into smaller ideas or topics you associate with it. Write each smaller idea, circle it, and draw a line connecting it to the center. Keep going—writing still more limited topics branching outward. You will end up with a cluster diagram like the one on the facing page.

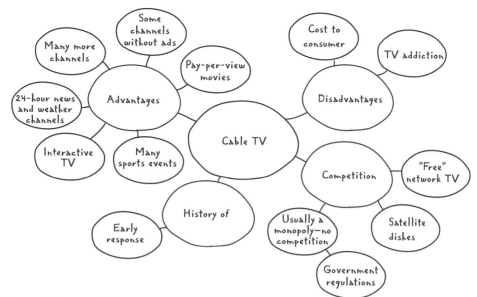

## 2 EXERCISE  Making a Cluster Diagram

In the space below, fill in a cluster diagram of one of the topics you came up with in Exercise 1. Remember: There are no right or wrong clusters. Start with the topic in the middle and branch out from there. Keep going until you run out of ideas and/or room.

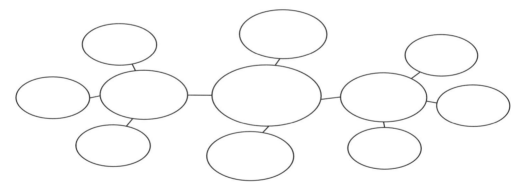

**Straight-line cluster.** Shown below is another kind of diagram that will help you limit a broad topic. It is a straight-line cluster that moves from broad, general subject (at the top) to ever more limited, narrower topics. Try it. You may find it more useful than the bigger cluster.

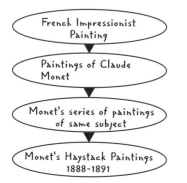

**HINT**

Your cluster diagram may look entirely different from those of your classmates, even though you all might start with the same broad, general subject. There are no "right" topics in a cluster diagram. A cluster records your own thoughts as you move from a general idea to narrower topics.

**EXERCISE 3**

## Limiting Your Topic

Fill in the straight-line diagram here. Start with a general topic and keep limiting it further and further. Your topic should "move" from the general at the top to the more and more limited as you approach the bottom. Make at least three of these diagrams, starting each one with a different topic.

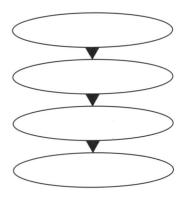

---

# Research Questions

 **Word your limited topic as a research question that you are going to investigate.**

Before you start exploring possible sources of information, spend a few minutes jotting down what you already know—or think you know—about your topic. This will help focus your research still further. As you take notes or freewrite, you may end up with one or more research questions— questions to which you would like to find the answers.

**Taking notes.** Here are some notes made by a student writer for a paper on reforms in the jury system in U.S. courts. The student wrote down everything she already knew and ended by focusing on the research question she wanted to explore.

*Courts use juries in trials to decide whether a person is innocent or guilty as accused. Both criminal and civil. Are there always 12 jurors?*

*Juries are supposed to be "jury of peers"—a mix of people who represent the population — of ages, races, gender. Are juries mentioned in U.S. Constitution?*

*How are people called to serve on juries, and what is the source of their names? I think maybe the lists of registered voters or in some places everyone with a driver's license. How old do you have to be?*

*Who actually gets to choose jurors—the lawyers? the judge?—and how are they chosen?*

*Cases of innocent people being convicted and guilty people going free.*

*I'd like to research proposed reforms (changes) in jury system. How can I find out?*

**Freewriting or Quickwriting.** Another way to find out what you already know is to quick-write or freewrite for a few minutes. Keep yourself focused on your topic, and just start writing. Don't worry about complete sentences or connections between ideas. The point is simply to get what's in your brain on paper (or on the computer monitor if you are using a word processor). A quick-write may contain information as well as questions. Because you think much faster than you write, use abbreviations, fragments—anything—to capture your thoughts as you focus on your topic.

*Research key words "jury reform" on WWW and on InfoTrac. See if I can interview Tony's mom, assistant state district attorney. I can write to natl or state Bar Assoc (organization of lawyers) & ask for info about jury reform. Maybe talk with Ben's older brother—graduated from law school last year & was editor of law review. Ask him for advice on how to research the topic—what are best sources?*

# Computer Connection

To freewrite on a computer, set a timer for five minutes and just keep writing. You might be able to concentrate better and think of more ideas if you are not watching what you write. Turn the brightness control all the way to dark; the screen will look blank. Then focus on your topic and keep writing until you run out of ideas. When you have finished, turn up the brightness control to see what you have written. Print your notes and save them.

**EXERCISE 4** Identifying Appropriately Limited Topics

For each numbered item below, identify the topics that are not too general and not too limited, but just right for a 5- to 7-page research paper. Write the letter of the topic you picked, and explain why you did not pick the others.

**1. a.** The population of the United States

   **b.** Information from the latest U.S. census

   **c.** Some problems in collecting accurate information in the latest U.S. census

   **d.** The number of people of Vietnamese origin living in San Francisco, according the latest census

   _____

   _____

   _____

**2. a.** Symbolism in Robert Frost's "Stopping by Woods on a Snowy Evening" and "Mending Wall"

   **b.** Robert Frost's poetry

   **c.** Symbolism in contemporary American poetry

   **d.** The origin of the word *wall*

   _____

   _____

   _____

**3. a.** Careers in medicine

   **b.** Pros and cons of being a nurse in a hospital emergency room

   **c.** The history of medicine in Europe during the twentieth century

   **d.** Medical research today

   _____

   _____

   _____

**4. a.** The career of Jackie Robinson, the first African American baseball player in the major leagues

    **b.** African Americans and baseball

    **c.** The history of baseball in America

    **d.** The World Series

_____

_____

_____

**EXERCISE 5**

## Limiting a Broad Subject

See how many limited topics, appropriate for a research paper you can list for each of the broad, general subjects below.

**EXAMPLE**
**General topic:** Dogs
**Limited topics:** Obedience training; breeds of dogs that are good with children; crime-fighting dogs; how seeing-eye dogs are trained; most dangerous dogs; animal shelters; rabies and other serious diseases; from wolves to dogs—their early history

**1.** Popular music

_____

_____

_____

_____

**2.** Space travel

_____

_____

_____

_____

**3.** Cartoons

_____

_____

_____

_____

**4.** World War II

_____

_____

_____

_____

## EXERCISE 6 Freewriting About a Limited Topic

Choose one of the limited topics you are considering for your paper. Freewrite for several minutes about what you already know about the topic, the questions you have, and any other thoughts or associations that come to mind. Remember, when you freewrite you don't have to write in complete sentences. Just stay focused on the limited topic and write down—as fast as you can—all of the thoughts, images, questions, and ideas that occur to you.

_____

_____

_____

_____

_____

_____

_____

_____

_____

_____

## EXERCISE 7 Revising Inappropriate Topics

Tell why each topic below is inappropriate for a research paper. Then suggest two alternative but related topics for each. Keep in mind the four requirements for a workable topic. (See pages 9–10.) For example:

INAPPROPRIATE: Snowboarding (too general)
WORKABLE: Dangers of snowboarding; comparing and contrasting water-skiing and snowboarding

**1.** My favorite Mexican foods

_____

_____

**2.** Space exploration in the year 2050

_____

_____

**3.** Airport security

_____

_____

**4.** American Indian art

_____

_____

**5.** Grammy awards

_____

_____

**6.** Hurricanes

_____

_____

**7.** William Shakespeare's plays

_____

_____

**8.** Slang in my grandmother's day

_____

_____

**9.** Chinese immigration to the United States

_____

_____

**10.** Solar energy

_____

_____

**EXERCISE** **Wording Your Research Questions**

For the limited topic that most interests you, write several research questions. These should simply be questions to which you would like to find the answers.

_____

_____

_____

_____

_____

_____

_____

_____

_____

_____

_____

**EXERCISE**

# Checking Your Progress

Answer each of the following questions.

**1.** What is the limited topic you have chosen to write about?

_____

_____

**2.** Are you satisfied with your research questions? Which one(s) appeal to you most?

_____

_____

**3.** What other topic ideas did you seriously consider? (Write your second and third choices.)

_____

_____

**4.** How or where did you get the idea for your limited topic?

_____

_____

**5.** Which approaches to finding and limiting your topic did you try?

_____

_____

**6.** Which approaches did you think were most useful?

_____

_____

## CHECKLIST REVIEW

☑ Make sure you understand your assignment.

☑ Choose a workable topic that meets all four requirements for a research paper topic.

1. You can find enough material on the topic.

2. The topic interests you, and you think you can make it interest your audience.

3. The topic is objective, not subjective.

4. The topic is limited enough to cover adequately in the space available.

☑ Word your limited topic as a research question that you are going to investigate.

# Locate Sources

It is now time to locate sources of information you will need for your research paper. In this chapter you will learn about the many resources available to you and how best to use them. Before setting out on Step 2, however, take a moment to check your progress against the timetable you have chosen as a model (see page 137). Remember, it's important to stay on schedule. Time lost or wasted now will be difficult—maybe impossible—to recover later.

## Two Kinds of Sources

As you begin to look for information about your topic, you will explore two kinds of sources: A **primary source** is an original text, document, interview, speech, or letter. It is not someone's comments on or analysis of a text; it is the text itself. A **secondary** source is *not* an original text or document but someone's comments on or analysis of a primary source. For example, U.S. Census data is a primary source. A study of economic trends based on Census data would be a secondary source.

### Here are some examples of primary and secondary sources.

**PRIMARY SOURCES:** Literary works (poems, stories, novels, essays, plays); documents; autobiographies; letters; interviews; speeches; surveys; tables of statistics

**SECONDARY SOURCES:** Comments on or analysis (either written or spoken) of an original text or document; biographies

Try to include at least one primary source in your paper. Your comments on a primary source will testify to your knowledge about your topic. Primary sources also provide a welcome change from reading about other people's ideas and opinions.

**Evaluate the sources that you find.**

**Check the date.** You will want accurate, up-to-date information, especially if the topic involves the sciences or social sciences. An article published in 1978 about space stations is seriously out of date, while a 1978 article about William Shakespeare could still be an excellent source. You will have to look at the article to see.

**Check the author.** Is the writer an expert on the topic? You can usually find some information about the writer (educational and career background) on a book's title page or jacket or at the beginning or end of a magazine article. Is there any indication that the writer is biased or unreliable? You need to be especially careful about using information you find on the Internet. (See page 22 on evaluating Internet sources.)

## Library/Media Center Resources

Libraries are often called **media centers** these days, and librarians are **media specialists**. That is because most libraries offer videos, audiocassette tapes, CDs, videodiscs, computer software, and electronic databases in addition to books, magazines, and newspapers.

**Start by exploring library resources.**

Remember that you need five or more good sources (or whatever number your teacher has specified), so allow yourself plenty of time to adjust your topic as you turn up new information or run into dead ends. Some sources may be dated; others may be unavailable; some may turn out not to contain any useful information on your topic.

**Use the card catalog to locate books in the library.** In some libraries, you will find the card catalog in rows of drawers containing index cards. Each book that the library owns has three different cards: these are filed by author, title, and subject. Many libraries have replaced these drawers of index cards with a user-friendly computer catalog that lets you search for books by author, title, and subject. You might also be able to conduct a **Boolean search**, a title search based on key words. After you enter two or more key words, the computer displays all of the book titles containing those key words. (See the examples below.) Ask your librarian to show you how to conduct one.

When you look up a book in the library's catalog, you will find its **call number**, the series of numbers and letters printed on the book's spine. A call number is like a road map; it tells you exactly where to find the

### BOOLEAN SEARCH

- For a search of myths about floods in cultures around the world, you might type these key words: *myth$* and *flood$*. (The symbol *$* lets you pull up titles with variant forms of the key word. In this case, you would get books about mythology and floods or flooding.)
- For a search of books about Willa Cather's *My Ántonia*, you would enter these key words: *cather.au.* and *my antonia.ti.* (The abbreviations *au.* and *ti.* stand for "author" and "title." The computer would list books about the novel *My Ántonia* written by Willa Cather.)

book you are looking for. Call numbers come from either the **Dewey Decimal System** or the **Library of Congress System** for classifying books by their subject. It is not necessary to memorize either system, but you do need to know that the call number of a nonfiction book indicates its general and specific subject and its author's last name. Nonfiction books are shelved according to their call numbers; books of fiction are shelved in a separate section, alphabetically by the author's last name.

**Use the reference section to find information and sources.** The library's reference section contains books and other materials that cannot be checked out. Here are some of the types of resources you can use.

**Encyclopedias.** Look up your topic in one or more of the standard multivolume encyclopedias, such as *World Book Encyclopedia*, *Encyclopedia Americana*, and *Encyclopaedia Britannica*. Your teacher may not accept encyclopedia articles as sources because they are too broad and general, but they will give you an overview of your topic. Also, at the end of many articles you will find useful bibliographies—lists of recommended books about the topic. Besides general encyclopedias, you may also find encyclopedias devoted to a single subject, such as *Grzimek's Animal Life Encyclopedia* and the *Great Artists of the Western World* series.

**Biographical information.** If you are tracking down information about a person, the reference section has many multivolume sources (such as *Contemporary Authors* and *Dictionary of Scientific Biography*). Some are published annually (such as *Who's Who in America* and *Current Biography*). You will also find specialized biographical sources (such as *Notable Native Americans*, *Notable Black American Women*, and *Who's Who in the Theatre*).

**Atlases.** These oversized books contain maps as well as geographical and economic information. There are historical atlases, showing past boundaries, and current atlases, showing nations, cities, and geographic features.

**Almanacs.** These single-volume books, published each year, are crammed with facts, charts, statistics, and other information.

**Dictionaries.** A reference section usually has one or more unabridged dictionaries—the oversized ones that contain nearly every word in the English language. There are specialized dictionaries, too, such as dictionaries of slang, sports terms, science, art, and foreign languages.

**Quotations.** Who said what, and when did he or she say it? If you are trying to track down the source of a familiar phrase or quotation or if you are looking for a quotation on a specific topic, you will find an assortment of books of quotations, such as *Bartlett's Familiar Quotations* and *The Home Book of Quotations*.

**Specialized books on all subjects.** The reference shelves are filled with many other books that librarians consider useful for research. You will find books about art history, science, math, and many other subjects. You will also find specialized indexes, such as *Book Review Digest*, *Granger's Index to Poetry*, *Short Story Index*, *Business Periodicals Index*, *Humanities Index*, and many others.

**Research aids.** If your topic is a current one, you can jump-start your research by using one of the mini-anthologies that provide articles, background information, and bibliographies about a current topic or issue. Check to see if your library has *Issues and Controversies on File*, *The CQ Researcher*, or *SirS Critical Issues*.

# Computer Connection

If it's okay with your teacher and you have access to a computer and modem, you can jump on the "information superhighway" to gather information. You will find it all on the **Internet**, a global network made up of smaller computer networks. Students at most colleges and universities have free access to the Internet, and in recent years government officials have vowed to make the Internet accessible in every school in the United States. Find out if a **Free-Net**, a community-based free access to the Internet, is available in your library. If it is, learn how to register for your own Free-Net account.

**Look for relevant newspaper and magazine articles.** Magazines and newspapers are called **periodicals**. You will find the current ones on library shelves. Back issues are usually stored on **microfilm** or **microfiche**. Before you search for magazine or newspaper articles about your topic, find out which periodicals are available in your library. The *Readers' Guide to Periodical Literature* indexes (by subject and author's last name—but not by title) articles in about 200 popular magazines. Paperback editions appear monthly and quarterly, and a cumulative hardbound edition is published each year. The following sample shows some typical entries as well as the many cross-references.

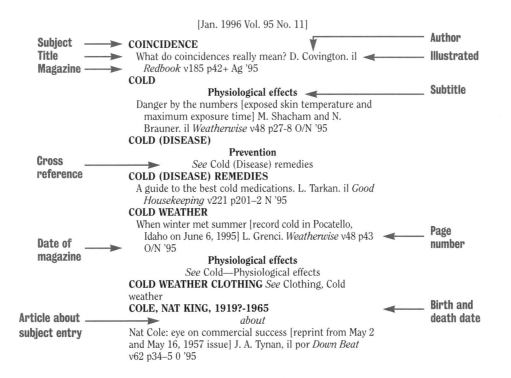

[Jan. 1996 Vol. 95 No. 11]

| Subject | COINCIDENCE |
| Title | What do coincidences really mean? D. Covington. il |
| Magazine | *Redbook* v185 p42+ Ag '95 |

Author
Illustrated

COLD

Physiological effects — Subtitle

Danger by the numbers [exposed skin temperature and maximum exposure time] M. Shacham and N. Brauner. il *Weatherwise* v48 p27-8 O/N '95

COLD (DISEASE)

Prevention

Cross reference — *See* Cold (Disease) remedies

COLD (DISEASE) REMEDIES

A guide to the best cold medications. L. Tarkan. il *Good Housekeeping* v221 p201–2 N '95

COLD WEATHER

When winter met summer [record cold in Pocatello, Idaho on June 6, 1995] L. Grenci. *Weatherwise* v48 p43 O/N '95 — Page number

Date of magazine

Physiological effects

*See* Cold—Physiological effects

COLD WEATHER CLOTHING *See* Clothing, Cold weather

COLE, NAT KING, 1919?-1965 — Birth and death date

Article about subject entry — *about*

Nat Cole: eye on commercial success [reprint from May 2 and May 16, 1957 issue] J. A. Tynan, il por *Down Beat* v62 p34–5 0 '95

**Computerized indexes.** InfoTrac, a computerized index, lets you search for newspaper and magazine articles by subject and author. It also gives an **abstract** (brief summary) of many articles. If you have access to InfoTrac on a computer database, you can also read and print whole articles.

**Vertical File.** A vertical file is really a file cabinet with folders filed alphabetically by topic—Careers, Crime, Hurricanes, Olympic Games, Peace Corps, and so on. The folders contain pamphlets, newspaper articles, government publications, and other materials pertaining to the topic.

## Computer Connection

Find out if your teacher will let you do some of your research on the World Wide Web. If you can use Internet sources in your paper, evaluate carefully whatever you find. Ask yourself these questions:

- **Who wrote the Web page?** Usually, you can find the name of the writer or organization (and sometimes an e-mail address) somewhere on the home page. How qualified or knowledgeable is the writer? Is the writer an expert or a professional working in the area the Web site discusses?
- **How accurate is the information?** Does the Web page give facts or just the writer's opinions? Verify factual information by locating the same facts in reliable print sources, such as encyclopedias or almanacs.
- **How up-to-date is the information?** Check the date on which the Web site was created and/or last updated.
- **Is the information biased (slanted toward one point of view), or are both sides of an issue presented objectively and fairly?** Bias is difficult to detect unless you know a lot about the topic or issue. Exaggeration, name-calling, and stereotyping are sure clues that the site is biased.

The biggest clue to a Web site's reliability is its **URL**, or **address**. Look for these **top-level domains** in the address:

- **.gov** indicates that the information is posted by a government agency or group and is generally reliable. For example, <http://www.census.gov> posts data from the U.S. Census Bureau.
- **.edu** is an educational source. A Web site with an *.edu* domain might have been created by someone in a second-grade class or someone associated with a college or university. A scholarly project at a university is almost always reliable, such as <http://www.xroads.virginia.edu>, which posts literary texts.
- **.org** is a nonprofit organization. The Web page of a museum is reliable, but look for bias in an organization sponsoring a cause.
- **.com** is a business. Be wary of information from businesses that are trying to sell you a product. Most major news organizations have reliable sites, such as <http://www.washingtonpost.com> and <http://www.cnn.com>.

    **.net** indicates a variety of organizations that offer Internet services.

## EXERCISE 1   Match That Source

For each item in Column A, write the letter in Column B

**COLUMN A**

_____ **1.** *Readers' Guide to Periodical Literature*

_____ **2.** atlas

_____ **3.** encyclopedia

_____ **4.** Internet

_____ **5.** Dewey Decimal System

_____ **6.** *Bartlett's Familiar Quotations*

_____ **7.** electronic database

_____ **8.** microfilm and microfiche

_____ **9.** periodical

_____ **10.** card catalog

**COLUMN B**

**a.** global network of com

**b.** book containing maps and information

**c.** index of articles in magazines and newspapers

**d.** books (either one or multiple volumes) containing alphabetically arranged articles on a wide range of subjects

**e.** statistics, facts, information, and articles accessed by computer

**f.** book of quotations

**g.** index of library's books (either online or on cards), indexed by subject, title, and author

**h.** system for classifying and shelving books

**i.** means of storing back issues of periodicals

**j.** publication issued at regular intervals (daily, weekly, monthly), such as a magazine, newspaper, or journal

## EXERCISE 2   Where Would You Look?

For each of the research questions listed below, write at least one sentence telling how you would look up information about the topic. What sources would you explore?

**1.** What are the latest research findings on the effects of dopamine, a chemical that transmits signals in the brain?

**2.** How do weather forecasters predict the force and track of hurricanes?

**3.** What is the history of Key West, the southernmost city in the continental United States?

**4.** What are some of the latest ideas on how to increase voter turnout, such as motor-voter registration (registering to vote when you get a driver's license) and voting by mail?

## ...Started

...you start gathering information for your report, brainstorm a list of library and computer resources that you might explore. Visit the library and start tracking down these sources, adding to your list as you research further. Next to each item on your list, note very briefly those sources that seem useful, those that do not, and why. (Continue your list on a separate sheet of paper if you need more room.)

_____

_____

_____

_____

_____

_____

_____

## Community Resources

**Find primary sources by exploring community resources.** Libraries and computers are not the only sources of information. Check out sources in your own community. Who knows a lot about or has had experience related to your topic? Where can you go to find information related to your topic? What questions would you ask an expert? You will create original primary sources as you write letters and conduct interviews and surveys.

**Write a letter to an expert.** If your topic is the migration pattern of monarch butterflies, you might write to a professor of entomology (the science of studying insects) at a local college or to a local resident who has a large butterfly collection.

Follow these guidelines when you write letters asking for information:

- Find out the person's name, title, and address, and follow the proper form for a business letter.
- Write your letter as soon as you can so that you allow enough time for a reply. (The problem with gathering information by writing letters is that you have no control over how quickly you will receive a reply.)
- Be polite and ask specific questions that show you already have some knowledge of your topic.
- If you receive a reply, write a short note thanking the person for the information you've received.

## EXERCISE 4 — Writing a Letter

Write a letter to someone who might provide you with information on the topic you are writing about. Find the name of the person, the person's complete address (including the ZIP code), and write the letter. You do not have to restrict yourself to people in your community; you can write to anyone who might have personal knowledge about your topic. Be sure to follow the proper form for a business letter. As a model you might use the letter shown here. It was written by the student author of the sample research paper printed in Step 10. She wrote to a person in her community who had direct experience of the historical event that was the topic of her paper.

```
1181 N.E. 172nd Street
North Miami Beach, FL 33162

November 22, 1995

Mr. Joseph Grunwald
2110 N.E. 207th St.
North Miami Beach, FL 33179

Dear Mr. Grunwald:

I am a 10th-grade student at North Miami Beach High
School, and I am writing a research paper about the
Cuban Missile Crisis of October 1962. I know from
your recent talk at our school about your experi-
ences during World War II that you were living in
Miami at the time of the Cuban Missile Crisis. I
have done a good deal of research into contemporary
newspaper accounts, and I would very much like to
interview you about your memories of what Miami was
like during the crisis.

I would expect the interview to last no more than
half an hour. It could be done at any time on the
weekend or any weekday evening at your convenience.
Please let me know whether you would be willing to
be interviewed about the Cuban Missile Crisis and,
if you are willing, when and where you would like
to schedule the interview.

I look forward to hearing from you.

Sincerely,

Leslie Porter
Leslie Porter
```

**Conduct an interview in person or on the telephone.** Instead of writing letters to ask questions, you might call or write someone knowledgeable about your topic to arrange for an interview. Follow these important steps:

- Before you get started, make sure that you have your teacher's permission for the interview.
- Either by letter or phone, explain to the interviewee who you are, what you are writing about, and why you think he or she might be helpful.
- Ask for a limited amount of time—perhaps 30 minutes—and set a definite time and day for the interview.
- Before the interview, prepare five to ten clearly worded questions that will yield specific information and guide the interview. Keep in mind that a prepared question may bring a reply that leads to other questions and answers. It is important to remain flexible enough to pursue unexpected leads.
- Appear (or call) promptly for the interview. Be polite and take notes. If you are going to tape-record the interview, ask for permission in advance.
- Ask for permission to use direct quotes from the interview in your paper.
- Don't overstay your welcome. Thank the person for his or her time, and send a follow-up letter of thanks.

**EXERCISE** **Preparing for an Interview**

Draft five questions you would ask each of the following persons in an interview on the topic given. Phrase your questions in a way that will encourage the person interviewed to respond with specific details. You might work with a partner to test your questions.

**1.** A famous sports figure (name him or her) on how to prepare for a career in his or her field.

**Name of person:** _____

_____

_____

_____

_____

_____

**2.** A local government official on juvenile crime (or any other serious issue) in your community.

**Name of person:** _____

_____

_____

_____

_____

_____

**3.** Your school principal (or a school board member or the superintendent of schools) on an education issue. (For example, curriculum, safety, budget, class size, educational reform, vocational education, dropouts, etc.)

**Name of person:** _____

_____

_____

_____

_____

_____

**Visit a local museum or government office.** You might sit in on a city council meeting or visit a local recycling plant. Is there nearby a museum related to your topic? You might find there exactly the information you need for your report. Check with the librarian or curator at the museum for help in tracking down the information you need. If you visit a government office, request publications or other information from a receptionist, who will steer you to the proper person.

## Focusing on Your Community

For each research question below, write a few sentences telling where and how you would find information in your community. List specific names and addresses, if possible.

**1.** What organized after-school athletic programs are available for elementary school boys and girls in your community?

_____

_____

_____

_____

**2.** What is your community doing or planning to do about recycling? How successful have recycling projects been during the last three years?

_____

_____

_____

_____

**3.** What specific resources does the community provide for senior citizens? What needs are not being met? How might the community meet these needs?

_____

_____

_____

_____

**4.** What is the procedure for deciding how local taxes are spent? What were last year's expenditures, and what is the proposed budget for the coming year?

_____

_____

_____

_____

**5.** What local organizations are available for people interested in the arts? Are there music groups, crafts groups, book groups?

_____

_____

_____

_____

**Conduct a survey.** When you conduct a survey, you have a chance to ask people everything you want to know about your topic. First, you will have to figure out a useful **sampling**, the group of people you will ask to complete your questionnaire. Then you will have to write clearly worded questions designed to elicit the information you are looking for. Instead of providing blank lines and asking people to write in their own answers to your questions, give them a choice of responses. This way it is easier to tally the results.

### Here is an example of a survey question and choice of responses

How many hours of television do you watch on an average weekday during the school year? (Include both daytime and evening viewing.)

&#10063; none    &#10063; less than 1    &#10063; 1–2 hours
&#10063; 2–3 hours    &#10063; 3–5 hours    &#10063; 6 or more hours

Creating a survey or questionnaire takes careful planning. Consider all of these questions:

■ Who will be your sampling and how many people will you survey? (The larger and more random the sample, the more accurate or representative your information will be. For example, instead of surveying just your close friends, you will get a more random sampling by surveying every other person in three or four homerooms at different grade levels.) How can you ensure that you will get enough responses?

■ Whose permission will you need to distribute your questionnaire?

■ What specific information do you want to find? Are your questions clearly worded? (You might try out your survey on several friends.) Are the responses designed so that they can be easily tallied?

■ What conclusions can you make based on the results of your survey?

**EXERCISE 7  Conducting a Survey**

Pretend that as part of your research paper on the TV-watching habits of students, you are going to conduct a survey. On the lines below or on a separate sheet of paper draft at least six questions with responses that can be easily tallied. Compare your questions with those of your classmates. You might create a class questionnaire and distribute it to other English classes. Tally the results, and decide what you can conclude from the survey.

_____

_____

_____

_____

_____

_____

## EXERCISE 8 — Go to It

Name one primary source that you plan to explore for your research paper: an interview, a letter, a visit, a survey. Detail the steps you will use, and compose whatever needs to be written. (Use a separate sheet of paper if you need more room.)

**a. Letter.** If you are writing a letter asking for information, find out the name, title, and address of a person who might provide the information. Draft the letter, revise it, and send it. Report to a classmate or classmates on the reply you receive.

**b. Interview.** Find out the name of a person you might interview. Draft ten questions you would ask that person. (Be sure to word your questions so that you get more than a yes or no answer.) Choose your best questions (at least six), and call or write to arrange for an interview. Be sure your teacher approves your interview plans.

**c. Survey.** Think of a survey that might help you gather useful information for your report. Who would take the survey? Draft a questionnaire (at least 7 or 8 questions with responses), revise it, and distribute it to your sample. Tally your results and decide what conclusions you can draw.

_____

_____

_____

_____

_____

_____

_____

_____

_____

_____

_____

## Bibliography Cards—Keeping Track of Sources

**Record complete information for every source you think you will use.**

For every source you consult, you will make a bibliography card on a 3" x 5" or 4" x 6" index card. On each card, you will record the author, title, and publishing information—and perhaps your own note or comment about the source. You will use these bibliography cards to create your "Works Cited" page, which lists all of the sources used in the paper. For this reason it is important to assign each card a source number (see the upper right-hand corner of each sample card shown on page 30). The source number will help you save time and keep track of where your notes come from.

**Book**

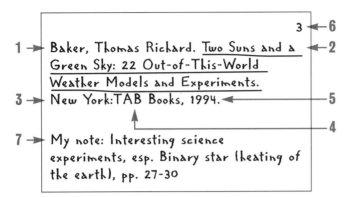

1 Author(s) or editor(s), last name first
2 Book's title, underlined
3 Place of publication
4 Publisher
5 Date of publication
6 Researcher's source number
7 Researcher's comment

**Newspaper or Magazine Article**

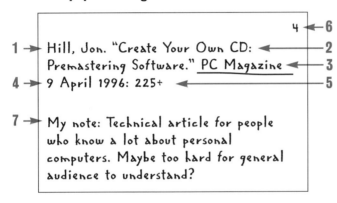

1 Author(s), if given
2 Article's title, enclosed in quotation marks
3 Newspaper's or magazine's title, underlined
4 Date of publication
5 Page(s) on which article appears
6 Researcher's source number
7 Researcher's comment

**Write each bibliography entry according to the style your teacher requires.** You will follow the exact same style when you write the entries for your Works Cited list , so getting the entries right on the bibliography source cards will save you a lot of time later. In the sample bibliography cards and the entries on pages 31–34, pay special attention to three things:

■ the information that is given
■ the order in which the information is given
■ the punctuation of each item

The entries in this chapter follow the **MLA (Modern Language Association) style** for documenting sources, which is the style most often required by high school and college teachers. A different style of documentation, the **APA (American Psychological Association) style**, is used in psychology journal articles and is required for college psychology papers (see Appendix B). Be sure to follow exactly the style of documentation your teacher requires.

## Computer Connection

With your teacher's permission, you might record source information on a computer instead of making bibliography cards. Create a bibliography document, and list each source's publishing information in the style shown on pages 31–34. With a click of the mouse, you can alphabetize your sources by selecting the Sort command from the Tools menu.

# MLA STYLE OF DOCUMENTING SOURCES

## BOOKS

### Book by a Single Author

Eddings, Joshua. How the Internet Works. Emeryville, CA: Ziff-Davis Press, 1994.

### Two or More Books by the Same Author

After the first mention of an author's name, use three hyphens followed by a period to indicate "same author as above."

Austen, Jane. Northanger Abbey. Ed. by Anne Henry Ehrenpreis. London: Penguin Classics, 1985.

—. Persuasion. Ed. by D.W. Harding. London: Penguin Classics, 1985.

### Book by Two Authors

Shroder, Tom, and John Barry. Seeing the Light: Wilderness and Salvation: A Photographer's Tale. New York: Random House, 1995.

### Book by Three or More Authors

You may either list all of the authors in the order in which they are listed on the title page, or you may list only the first author followed by the abbreviation *et al.* ("and others"). Either style is acceptable. Find out which one your teacher prefers.

Brownstein, Samuel C., Mitchel Weiner, and Sharon Weiner Green. How to Prepare for the SAT Scholastic Aptitude Test. 14th ed. New York: Barron's, 1987.

Greenough, Sarah, et al. On the Art of Fixing a Shadow: One Hundred and Fifty Years of Photography. Washington, DC: National Gallery of Art, 1989.

### Book by a Single Editor

Washington, Martha, ed. Narrative of Sojourner Truth. New York: Vintage, 1993.

### Book by Single Author with Editors and Translator

Frank, Anne. The Diary of a Young Girl: The Definitive Edition. Ed. Otto H. Frank and Mirjam Pressler. Trans. Susan Massotty. New York: Doubleday, 1995.

### Book by Two Editors

Goldhammer, Arthur, and Christine Klapish-Zuber, eds. A History of Women in the West, Vol. 2: Silences of the Middle Ages. Cambridge, MA: Belknap Press, 1994.

### Book by Three or More Editors

Perkins, George, Barbara Perkins, and Phillip Leininger, eds. Benét's Reader's Encyclopedia of American Literature. New York: HarperCollins, 1991.

### Book with No Author Cited

The Baseball Encyclopedia. 8th ed. New York: Macmillan, 1990.

### Book That Is Part of a Series

Women Writers. Great Writers of the English Language Ser. Freeport, New York: Marshall Cavendish, 1989.

### Multivolume Work

Draper, James P., et al., eds. <u>Contemporary Literary Criticism</u>. Vol. 84. New York: Gale Research, 1995.

### Edition

Lincoln, C. Eric. <u>The Black Muslims in America</u>. 3rd ed. Trenton, NJ: Africa World Press, 1994.

### Translation

Appelfeld, Aharon. <u>To the Land of the Cattails</u>. Trans. Jeffrey M. Green. New York: Harper & Row, 1987.

### Government Publication

United States. U.S. General Accounting Office. <u>Student Testing: Current Extent and Expenditures, with Cost Estimates for a National Examination</u>. Washington, DC: GAO, 1993.

### Pamphlet

Stevenson, George B. <u>Trees of Everglades National Park and the Florida Keys</u>. 2nd ed. 1969.

## PARTS OF BOOKS

### Story, Essay, Poem, or Play in an Anthology

Hurston, Zora Neal. "Drenched in Light." <u>The Portable Harlem Renaissance Reader</u>. Ed. David Levering Lewis. New York: Viking, 1994. 691-698.

García Márquez, Gabriel. "A Very Old Man with Enormous Wings." Trans. Gregory Rabassa. <u>Collected Stories</u>. New York: Harper and Row, 1984. 203-210.

### Introduction, Foreword, or Preface
#### *By the Author of the Work*

Porter, Katherine Anne. "Go Little Book . . ." Preface. <u>The Collected Stories of Katherine Anne Porter</u>. New York: Harcourt Brace, 1965. v-vi.

#### *By Someone Other than the Author of a Work*

Baldwin, James. "Sweet Lorraine." Introduction. <u>To Be Young, Gifted and Black</u>. By Lorraine Hansberry, adapted by Robert Nemiroff. Englewood Cliffs, NJ: Prentice Hall, 1969. ix-xii.

### Article in an Encyclopedia or Other Reference Book
#### *Unsigned*

For a familiar reference work, you do not have to cite the city and publisher. Articles from less familiar reference books should have full publishing information (city of publisher and publisher).

"Islamic Art and Architecture." <u>Columbia Encyclopedia</u>. 5th ed. 1993.

"Dominican Republic." <u>Statesman's Year-Book, 1995-96</u>. 132nd ed. Ed. Brian Hunter. New York: St. Martin's Press, 1995. 492-496.

#### *Signed*

Bevan, Clifford. "Trumpet." <u>The New Grove Dictionary of Jazz</u>, Vol. 2. Ed. Barry Kernfeld. New York: Macmillan, 1988. 555-558.

## MAGAZINE AND NEWSPAPER ARTICLES
### Magazine Article

Notice how the date (day of month followed by abbreviated month) and page numbers are cited. Do not cite volume or issue numbers. A plus sign (+) indicates that the article begins on that page and is continued on the following pages, which are not consecutive.

Finnegan, William. "The New Americans." <u>New Yorker</u> 25 Mar. 1996: 52-71.

Preston, Douglas, and Christine Preston. "The Granddaddy of the Nation's Trails Began in Mexico." <u>Smithsonian</u> Nov. 1995: 140+.

### Newspaper Article

Greenhouse, Linda. "Supreme Court Roundup: Justices to Review Arizona's Law Making English Its Official Language." New York Times 26 Mar. 1996, southern ed., sec. 1: 10.

### Newspaper Editorial

"Social Security System Needs an Overhaul Now." Editorial. USA Today 19 Mar. 1996, late ed., sec. 1: 12.

### Newspaper Column

Glassman, James K. "Jobs: The (Woe Is) Me Generation." Editorial. Washington Post 19 Mar. 1996: A 17.

### Letter to the Editor

Fones, Zeta. "Benefits of Vitamin E." Saturday Evening Post Jan./Feb. 1996: 6.

## ELECTRONIC SOURCES

### Online Magazine Article

Landsburg, Steven E. "Grade Expectations." Slate Magazine 11 Aug. 1999.  12 Jan. 2000. <http://www.slate.com/Economics/99-08-11/Economics.asp>.

### Online Newspaper Article

Associated Press. "Freeing Willy, in Real Life." 8 Sept. 1999. New York Times on the Web. 22 Dec. 1999. <http://search.nytimes.com/>.

### Online Reference Work

Tufts, Eleanor. "Mary Cassatt." Grolier's Academic American Encyclopedia, 1994. Online. CompuServe. 19 Sept. 1996.

### Scholarly Project

The Avalon Project. Yale U Law School 2 June 1999. <http://www.yale.edu/lawweb/avalon/diplomacy/forrel/cuba/cubamenu.htm>.

### Professional Web Site

"Adult CPR/AED Training." The American National Red Cross. 3 Feb. 2000. <http://www.redcross.org.hss.cpraed.html>.

### Posting to a Newsgroup or Forum

Graffis, Mark. "Whales, Dolphins at Risk from Canaries Ferry." Online posting. 4 Aug. 1999. Issues: Whales. 28 Sept. 1999. <http://www.deja.com>.

### E-mail

Futscher, Vicki. Office of the Historian, Bureau of Public Affairs. 27 July 1999. E-mail to the author.

### CD-ROM Encyclopedia Article

"Antarctica." Complete Reference Collection. CD-ROM. The Learning Company, 1997.

## OTHER SOURCES

### Television or Radio Program

Evening News with Peter Jennings. ABC. WPLG, Miami. 12 Feb. 1996.

### Sound Recording (Tape, CD, LP)

Webber, Andrew Lloyd. "The Old Gumble Cat." Cats: Selections from the Original Broadway Cast Recording. Cond. Stanley Lewebowsky. Geffen, 9 2026-2, 1983. Based on T.S. Eliot's Old Possum's Book of Practical Cats.

### Film or Video Recording

Moyers, Bill, dir. Maya Angelou. Creativity ser. PBS Home Video, New York: CEL Communications, 1991.

The Grapes of Wrath. Dir. John Ford. With John Carradine, Jane Darwell, and Henry Fonda. Writ. Nunnally Johnson. Twentieth Century-Fox, 1940.

### Performance (Concert, Play, Opera, Ballet)

To Be Young, Gifted and Black. By Lorraine Hansberry. Dir. Gene Frankel. With Barbara Baxley, Rita Gardner, Janet League, Cicely Tyson, John Beal, Gertrude Jeanette, Stephen Strimpell, Andre Womble. Cherry Lane Theatre, New York. 2 Jan. 1969.

### Work of Art

Hopper, Edward. Office in a Small City. Metropolitan Museum of Art, New York.

**Interview**

*Published Interview*

Drossos, George. Interview. <u>Division Street America</u>. By Studs Terkel. New York: Pantheon, 1967. 93-96.

*Unpublished Interview*

Balsameda, Liz. Personal interview. 28 Nov. 1996.

**Letter**

*Published Letter*

Crane, Stephen. "To Joseph Conrad." 17 Mar. 1898. Letter 228 in <u>Stephen Crane: Letters</u>. Ed. R.W. Stallman and Lillian Gilkes. New York: New York UP, 1960. 176-77.

*Unpublished Letter*

Clinton, Bill, President. Letter to the author. 11 Feb. 1996.

**Map or Chart**

Texas. Map. Skokie, IL: Rand, 1995. 228-231.

**Cartoon**

Adams, Scott. Cartoon. Miami Herald [Miami] 27 Mar. 1996: 6D.

**Lecture, Speech, or Address**

Henry, Patrick. "Liberty or Death." Speech before the Virginia Convention. 23 Mar. 1775.

Kennedy, John F. Inaugural address. Washington, DC 20 Jan. 1961.

## EXERCISE 9  Preparing Bibliography Source Card Entries

Write a bibliography source card entry for each of the following items, using the MLA style shown in the preceding pages. Be sure to give the information in the proper order and use the correct punctuation.

**1.** Ellen [first name] Paul wrote a book about adoption called *Adoption Choices*. It was published in 1991 by Gale Research in the city of Detroit.

**2.** Bryan Bunch and Alexander Hellemans are the two authors of a book called *The Timetables of Technology*. Their publisher is Simon & Schuster, located in New York. The book appeared in 1993.

**3.** Jay Hyams is the translator and Giovanni [first name] Pinna is the author of a book about fossils. Its title is *The Illustrated Encyclopedia of Fossils*. It was published in 1990 by Facts on File in New York.

**4.** *Life* magazine published a special edition of its magazine in 1969, the year when a human being first set foot on the moon. Dora Jane Hamblin's article is titled "Neil Armstrong: He could fly before he could drive." This special edition of *Life* has no page numbers, no month and day—only the year.

## EXERCISE 10

# What Is Wrong with These Bibliography Source Card Entries?

Each of the following bibliography source card entries contains at least one error; some contain many errors. Rewrite each entry, following exactly the MLA style as described above. Check carefully the punctuation, the information included, and the order of information.

**1.** Ralph Hickok. <u>A Who's Who of Sports Champions</u>. Houghton Mifflin, New York, 1995.

_____

_____

_____

**2.** Editors, Francine Tenenbaum, Rita Buchanan, Roger Holmes. <u>Taylor's Master Guide to Gardening</u>. Boston, Houghton Mifflin. 1994.

_____

_____

_____

**3.** Allende, Isabel. <u>Paula</u>. Translated by Margaret Sayers Peden. 1994, HarperCollins: New York.

_____

_____

_____

**4.** Hahn, Harley. <u>The Internet Yellow Pages, Third edition</u>. Berkeley, CA, McGraw Hill. 1996. 3rd edition.

_____

_____

_____

**5.** French, Howard W. "For Ivory Coast Women, New Battle for Equality" in New York Times, a newspaper, Apr. 6 1996, page 4, southern edition.

_____

_____

_____

**6.** Jerome, Marty. "Printers Get Personal." <u>PC Computing</u>, a magazine. Feb. 1996. Pages 140, 142–144, 146, 148, 150–152, 156.

_____

_____

_____

## Exploring Sources

List every source that you explore as you do research for your paper. (Use a separate sheet of paper if you think you will need more room.) Follow exactly the MLA style for documenting sources, as shown on pages 31–34. Write a bibliography card for each source that you think will be useful.

_____

_____

_____

_____

_____

_____

_____

_____

_____

_____

_____

_____

_____

_____

_____

_____

## CHECKLIST REVIEW

☑ Evaluate the sources that you find.

☑ Start by exploring library resources.

  1. Use the card catalog to locate books in the library.

  2. Use the reference section to find information and sources.

  3. Look for relevant newspaper and magazine articles.

☑ Find primary sources by exploring community resources.

  1. Write a letter to an expert.

  2. Conduct an interview in person or on the telephone.

  3. Visit a local museum or government office.

  4. Conduct a survey with a questionnaire.

☑ Record complete information for every source you think you will use.

☑ Write each bibliography entry according to the style your teacher requires.

# Take Notes

BIG NATE reprinted by permission of Newspaper Enterprise Association, Inc.

**N**ow that you have tracked down your sources, you are about to start the task of gathering information for your research paper. Note-taking is a crucial step on the way to your finished paper. If you do a good job taking notes, all the rest of the steps in completing your research paper will be a lot easier. But if you are lax and careless—if, for example, you do not take care to record and credit your sources fully and accurately—you will make more work for yourself later on.

## Working Outline

**Before you start taking notes, make a working outline.**

Stop to make a plan—a road map to see where you are headed. Like all outlines, a working outline lists main topics and subtopics in some kind of logical order, but a working outline is informal and definitely not final. (You will make your final outline later.) Its purpose is to guide your research and note-taking. The following questions will help you plan your working outline.

- What are my research questions—the questions I want to find the answers to?

- What are the most important ideas I want to cover in my paper?

- What background information will readers need to have?

- What are the main parts, or sections, of my paper, and how do they relate to one another?

- How might I best organize the information?

- What conclusion(s) do I expect to make?

You will probably revise your working outline several times as you take notes and think about your paper. You may decide to drop, add, change, or rearrange topics and subtopics as you discover—or are unable to find—the information that you are looking for.

On the following page is an example of a working outline for a paper about the World Wide Web.

```
How to Create a Home Page for the World Wide Web
   I. What a home page is (background information)
     A. World Wide Web
        1. Its history
        2. Its purpose
     B. Purpose of a home page
        1. To share information
        2. To sell something
        3. Other purposes?
     C. Who has home pages? (give some examples)
        1. Companies
        2. Cities, universities, government agencies
        3. Private individuals
  II. How to design a home page
     A. Software to use (Web Wizard, Web Weaver, Hot Dog)
     B. Graphics companies do it for you
 III. How to register a home page and get it on-line
     A. Using a Web server
     B. Getting an address
     C. Paying a fee
```

## EXERCISE 1  Making a Working Outline for Your Paper

On the lines below or on a separate sheet of paper, write a working outline for your research paper. Think about the main ideas you want to cover and how best to arrange them. Remember that you will probably revise this working outline as you continue to research and take notes.

_____

_____

_____

_____

_____

_____

_____

_____

_____

_____

_____

_____

_____

_____

_____

 **Skim your sources to locate information for your paper.**
Skimming is the very fast type of reading you use when you search for specific information or for a particular kind of information.

Here's how to skim for information if your source is a book:

- Turn to the index (if there is one) at the back of the book or to the table of contents at the front. Look for headings related to your topic and research questions.

- When you find a heading that seems useful, turn to the page(s) listed and skim to see if that page or section of the book has the information you want.

- Force your eyes to move very quickly until you find the information you want or decide that it is not there.

To skim a newspaper, magazine, or encyclopedia article, read each subhead and quickly glance at the paragraphs, paying special attention to the first and last sentences of each.

Not every source you explore will have useful information. Don't waste time reading a source slowly or taking notes once you have decided the source isn't useful.

## Practice Skimming to Locate Information

**EXERCISE 2**

Force yourself to read at top speed as you look for specific information. Use a daily newspaper to do this exercise.

**1.** What program is playing tonight on NBC at 8 P.M.? If you watch television tonight at 8 P.M., what program will you choose to watch? What channel is it on?

_____

_____

**2.** What is the main subject of each of the editorials on the editorial page?

_____

_____

**3.** In one sentence, summarize the most important story in today's newspaper. (A newspaper's most important story is usually in the upper-right-hand column of the front page of the first section.)

_____

_____

**4.** Write the headline and the name of the author of a story that appears in the sports section. Then summarize the story in one sentence.

_____

_____

_____

_____

## Skimming One of Your Sources

Skim one of the sources you have listed on page 36 to see if you can find information that is directly related to the topic of your paper. Write the topic as it is listed in the source and the page number(s) on which the information is located. Circle all of the page numbers that contain information you think will be useful enough for you to take notes. (NOTE: When you are checking the rest of your sources, you won't write this information down or circle page numbers. You will start taking notes on note cards as soon as you locate useful information.)

1. Title and author of source _____

_____

_____

2. Information related to (name of topic) _____

_____

3. Page number(s) where information is located _____

_____

_____

## Taking Notes on Note Cards

When you find information that you think will be useful for your paper, it's time to adjust your reading speed. Slow down from skimming speed to the pace you use when you are trying to understand information. If you are like most readers, that means you will read every sentence, not skipping any words, and concentrate on the meaning of what you are reading. You still will not take notes on everything you find—just on information that you think might be useful for your paper.

**Take notes in your own words. Enclose a direct quotation (the author's exact words) in quotation marks.**

In your finished paper, you must not copy the words or ideas of another writer without giving that writer credit. You cannot even come _close_ to copying. If you do, you are guilty of **plagiarism**: stealing another person's words and/or ideas and passing them off as your own. Plagiarism, which comes from a Latin word meaning "kidnapper," is totally unacceptable. It is a very serious academic offense and carries very serious consequences. So when you take notes, you have to do something to ensure that you will be able to distinguish your own words and thoughts from an author's. (See numbers 5 and 6 in the following guidelines.)

### Follow these eight guidelines for taking notes:

**1.** Use 3" x 5" cards or 4" x 6" cards. (Or you can cut pieces of paper to either of these sizes.)

**2.** Write the source number in the upper-right-hand corner of the card. On each card take notes from only one source.

**3.** Write on only one side of each card, and write about only one main idea. (You will then be able to arrange and rearrange your note cards easily according to their main ideas.)

**4.** Write a heading—a key word or phrase—at the top of the note card and underline it. The heading tells the main idea discussed on the note card. Usually, the heading is one of the topics or subtopics in your working outline.

**5.** Make a conscious effort to use your own words when you take notes. It may help to close the book and explain to yourself what the author has written, then transfer that "explanation" to your note card. You do not need to write in complete sentences. Use abbreviations and symbols.

**6.** Enclose direct quotations in large quotation marks. Make sure you have quoted word for word, *exactly* as the author wrote it. If you wish to leave out any material from the quoted passage—a sentence or phrase or even a single word—you must show that you have done so by inserting ellipses at the appropriate point. (For more information on ellipses and other changes to quoted material, see Step 6.)

**7.** At the bottom of each note card, write the page number(s) where you found the information.

**8.** Before you go on to a new note card, double-check to see that you have written the source number and page numbers. If you haven't done this, your note card will be useless because you will not be able to find and document the source of your information again.

EXAMPLE

heading → <u>What mountain climbers need</u>    4 ← source number
Interview w. Sir Edmund Hillary (first to climb Mt.Everest, 5/29/53):
1. Strong motivation
2. Technical skill
3. Good planning
4. Sense of humor

p. 65 ← page number in source

# Computer Connection

If you are lucky enough to have the use of a laptop, you can take it with you to the library (or any other place you visit to find information) and take notes directly on the computer. Or if you have access to a PC or word processor at school or at home, you can also keyboard your notes. Save your notes in a separate file or document and be sure to print out a hard copy—just in case something happens to the file or to the computer.

You can make sorting through your notes (the first job in Step 4) a lot easier if you group all the notes with the same heading (key word or phrase at the top of the note card). Here's how to do it. Write your heading and then hit the Search or Find command in the Edit menu. Search for that same heading elsewhere in your notes. If you find another note with the same heading, write your new notes in the same place. Then, when you print your notes, you will have them neatly grouped by heading.

## Three Kinds of Notes

Your notes will probably contain a mixture of direct quotations, paraphrases, and summaries.

**Direct quotations.** Sometimes you will find a writer's wording so vivid or effective that you decide you might want to quote it in your paper. On your note card, copy the quote exactly—word for word—just as the writer wrote it, and enclose the quoted material in large quotation marks. (The "jumbo" quotes will alert you immediately that the wording isn't yours.)

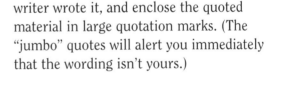

> **HINT**
>
> In your finished paper, keep direct quotations brief and use them sparingly. Think of sprinkling a handful or two of direct quotations throughout your paper. No more than one-fifth of your total paper should be direct quotations.

**EXERCISE 4**

## Taking Notes for a Direct Quotation

Look through one of your sources until you find a sentence or phrase you might quote directly in your paper. Fill out a note card for that direct quotation.

**Paraphrasing.** When you paraphrase a text, you restate the writer's ideas in your own words. A paraphrase covers every idea in the same order as in the original but is usually shorter. Paraphrases are most useful when you are writing about a short literary text, such as a poem. See if you can recognize this poem from its paraphrase:

> The speaker in the poem remembers a time when he was walking in the autumn woods and came to a place where he had to choose between two roads. He stood there a long time, feeling sad that he could not travel both. After peering down one road as far as he could see, he chose the other, grassier one. Both roads were worn about the same and were covered with fresh leaves. He told himself he would go down the other road someday but didn't really think he would ever be back. He says that he will be telling about this choice many years in the future. His taking the less-traveled road was an important turning point in his life.
>
> (The poem is Robert Frost's "The Road Not Taken.")

Suppose you are paraphrasing a writer's ideas from one of your sources. Even though you are not copying the writer's exact words, you are "kidnapping" the writer's ideas, and unless you give credit to the original writer, you are plagiarizing.

It is not enough simply to mention in passing that information you are presenting in your paper is paraphrased from the work of another author. The acknowledgment must be formal: a parenthetical reference to the original source, which is listed on the Works Cited page. (Rules and guidelines for documenting sources are covered in Step 7.) In the example that follows, note that the writer not only refers to the book and the author who is being paraphrased (*Cosmos*, by Carl Sagan) but also cites the page number where the original material is located in that book. (Since the book title is given in the passage, the writer need only cite the page.) Had the writer failed to credit the original author in this fashion, he or she would be guilty of plagiarism.

> In <u>Cosmos</u>, based on his thirteen-part television series, Carl Sagan describes the extraordinary "songs" of whales and dolphins. Because sight and smell are not much use in cloudy ocean waters, Sagan explains, these underwater mammals communicate by means of sound. Humpback whales have extraordinary memories, and scientists have recorded exact repetitions of whale "songs" that last anywhere from 15 minutes to an hour. Sometimes groups of whales sing in unison. They are clearly communicating, but no one has figured out what the songs mean (271).

## 5 EXERCISE  Paraphrasing

Choose an important paragraph from one of your sources. Write a paraphrase on the lines below or on a separate piece of paper. With a partner, compare your paraphrase with the original text. Have you included all of the writer's ideas in the same order as in the original? Have you used *your own* words? Have you credited the original source? (Make up a source number and cite it in parentheses.)

_____

_____

_____

_____

_____

**Summarizing.** When you summarize something, you restate the main ideas in your own words. A summary does not give all the details—only the most important ones. Here, for example, are several paragraphs about utopias, followed by a brief summary.

ORIGINAL TEXT:

> Do you think you would like to live in a utopia? The word *utopia* is a made-up word that means, literally, "not a place." Sir Thomas More made up the word from the ancient Greek *ou-* (not) and *topos* (a place). More, a prominent English author and statesman, described the island of Utopia in a political essay in 1516. In More's *Utopia*, men and women are equally educated (unheard of at the time), and all religions are tolerated. More's Utopia is an ideal society in which every person thrives and injustice, poverty, and misery no longer exist. More's *Utopia*, published in Latin, was an immediate success. Unfortunately for More, his conflict with King Henry VIII over Henry's desire to break from the Roman Catholic church led to More's beheading in 1535.

> Gradually, the words *utopia* and *utopian* have come to refer to any ideal society. Since More's day, other writers have written about such societies, most notably Samuel Butler in *Erewhon* (1872), an anagram of the word *nowhere*, and Edward Bellamy in *Looking Backward* (1888). B.F. Skinner's *Walden Two* (1961) depicts an ideal community based on the writer's behavioral psychology theories. All of these utopian works criticize contemporary society and propose remedies for society's ills. Satires of utopian societies abound, including Jonathan Swift's *Gulliver's Travels* (1726), Aldous Huxley's *Brave New World* (1932), and George Orwell's *1984* (1949). The latter two portray *dystopias*, societies in which something is vastly wrong.

SUMMARY:

> The word *utopia* comes from the ideal society Sir Thomas More
> described in a political essay in 1516. More called his island Utopia,
> from the Greek for "not a place." Utopian literature does two things:
> criticizes what is wrong with the writer's society and suggests ways
> to fix society's injustices and other problems. Other utopian novels
> include Bellamy's *Looking Backward*, Butler's *Erewhon*, and
> Skinner's *Walden Two*. Swift's *Gulliver's Travels*, Huxley's *Brave
> New World*, and Orwell's *1984* are satires of utopias.

Keep in mind that when you are taking notes, you do not have to use complete sentences. Words, phrases, and fragments are fine—just as long as you can understand later what you have written on your note card and you make sure to avoid plagiarism.

EXAMPLE

```
Meaning of utopia                    2
Utopia (Gr., "not a place"). Made up by
Sir Thomas More, name of island & ideal
society in his essay Utopia (1516). Utopia
& utopian = any ideal society

                            p. 426
```

If you have photocopied your source (a newspaper or magazine article, for instance), you can highlight main ideas with a brightly colored, transparent marker. Then when you make your note cards, you can go directly to the highlighted parts of the article.

 **EXERCISE 6 Summarizing Important Information from a Source**

Choose one of the sources that you plan to use for your research paper. On note cards, summarize each of the important ideas that may be of use to you, using your own words. Be sure to write a heading, the source number (see your bibliography cards), and the page number on which you found your information.

 **EXERCISE 7 Practice Taking Notes**

Here is a brief passage on the first African American baseball player in the major leagues. Use the lines that follow to take notes in your own words. The purpose of your research is to answer the research questions: Who was the first African-American baseball player in the major leagues? What happened to him? Compare your notes with those of a partner or small group.

> When World War II ended, some people, including reporters, argued
> that Black Americans had fought and died in the war and that it was
> time to integrate professional baseball. Branch Rickey, the Brooklyn
> Dodgers' president, agreed. He assigned Dodger scouts to search for
> a talented player in the Negro leagues. Rickey chose Jackie
> Robinson, who was playing shortstop for the Kansas City Monarchs.

According to Rickey's plan, Robinson would play for a year with a Canadian team, the Montreal Royals, the Dodgers' best minor league team. In 1946, he led the league in batting and runs scored, and that year the Royals won the pennant and the Little World Series. The grateful Montreal fans considered him a hero.

On April 10, 1947, Rickey announced that Robinson would become the first African American player in the major leagues. That first season Robinson and his wife received hate mail and death threats. He and his teammates were jeered by fellow baseball players and managers and by fans. And Robinson was turned away from hotels and restaurants that accommodated his teammates. But Robinson never lost his cool, and he played extraordinary baseball that season. Lightning fast, he led the league in stolen bases. His 12 home runs, 175 hits, and great fielding at first base led to his being named Rookie of the Year. Robinson was named the Most Valuable Player in 1949, the year he stole 37 bases and led the league in batting.

When he was inducted into the Baseball Hall of Fame in 1962, Robinson said, "I feel quite inadequate to this honor. It is something that could never have happened without three people. Branch Rickey was as a father to me, my wife, and my mother. They are here making the honor complete." He became the first baseball player—black or white—to have his portrait on a U.S. postage stamp.

_____

_____

_____

_____

_____

_____

_____

_____

_____

_____

_____

_____

## Practice Taking Notes During an Interview

Pretend that you have been asked to introduce a classmate at a school assembly. Interview a classmate about his or her earliest memories, family, hobbies, ambitions, etc. Think of five or six questions, and take notes on your classmate's responses. Introduce your classmate to the class, using the notes you took during your interview.

**EXERCISE** ## Taking Notes for Your Research Paper

In each of the possible sources you have discovered, skim until you locate information you think will be useful in your research paper. Then take notes, following the guidelines on page 41. You may end up with dozens of cards from each source. Before you leave each card, double-check to see that you have written the correct source number in the upper-right-hand corner and that you have listed the page numbers where you found the information.

---

### CHECKLIST REVIEW

☑ Before you start taking notes, make a working outline.

☑ Skim each source to locate information for your paper.

☑ Take notes in your own words.

☑ Enclose a direct quotation (the author's exact wording) in quotation marks.

☑ Follow the guidelines for taking notes on page 41.

# Write a Thesis Statement and a Title

CALVIN AND HOBBES ©1989 Watterson. Dist. By UNIVERSAL PRESS SYNDICATE. Reprinted with permission. All rights reserved.

**Y**ou have finished—or at least you think you've finished—taking notes. You have hundreds of note cards. What's next? You will be happy to know that the next few tasks are much easier than the ones you have already completed. You are now about halfway through the job of writing a research paper. Check your progress against the schedule you have set for yourself.

## Organizing and Evaluating Your Note Cards

Before you write a thesis statement and a title for your paper, you will need to pay some attention to your note cards.

### Sort your note cards into stacks having the same heading.

Some stacks will be short; some may be quite tall. If you have a great many cards under one heading, perhaps you should divide them into two or three more manageable subheadings.

Take time to reread each note card as you sort your cards. Make sure that you have got the heading right. You may find cards that might better be classified under different headings.

### Evaluate your note cards.

If you stopped to read and evaluate information *before* you took notes from your sources, you probably will not have ended up with many unusable note cards. Some students, however, can't resist capturing every scrap of information that might just *possibly* turn out to be useful. Now is the time to get rid of what you are sure you will not use.

**Be selective.** Do you have too much information on one subject? Use only the best—the most interesting, the most pertinent, the most persuasive. But do not destroy or throw away the weaker note cards—you may need them yet. Instead, place them at the bottom of the piles, and mark them in some way (maybe a small red X) so that when you start writing, you will recognize these cards as weaker than the others.

**Fill in the gaps.** Is there not enough information (not enough cards) in some stacks? Go back to the library, find more sources, and take additional notes.

**Revise your outline.** Revise your working outline to fit the information you have found. Consider eliminating topic(s) for which you have not been able to find information.

**What's this doing here?** If you have no idea

why a note card made it into a particular pile, move it to a more suitable pile or drop it altogether. You might make a separate pile of possible discards.

You should end up with a stack of note cards for each heading and subheading in your working outline. If you don't have at least two cards for each section of the outline, you may not have enough information.

## Unity

**Make sure that all of your information fits the scope of your paper.**
Think of the paper's **scope** as a big umbrella that covers all of the paper's main ideas and supporting details. Information that strays outside the paper's scope distracts the read-

er and destroys the paper's **unity**. As you reread and evaluate your notes, you will develop an even clearer idea of exactly what you are writing about. If you suspect that a note card does not belong under the umbrella, pull it out and set it aside.

**For a research paper on the effects of day care on children under two years old, which of the following studies fit the paper's scope?**

**1.** A study of children under the age of two who spend at least 20 hours a week in day-care centers in Houston, Texas.

**2.** A recent study of the training, qualifications, and experience of day-care workers in New York City.

**3.** A study of the personalities, development, and sleeping habits of 3,000 babies aged two or under and who spend more than 10 hours a week in day care.

**4.** A study of the personality differences in one-year-old identical twins in southern California.

The first and third studies fit the paper's stated scope. The second and fourth studies do not. Study 2 is about day-care workers, not children in day care. Although study 4 deals with one-year-olds, it does not specify that these children are in day care.

## EXERCISE 1 — What Fits and What Doesn't?

Put a check mark in the blank for the items of information that fit the research paper described. Write an X for the items that do not fit and will hurt the paper's unity.

For a research paper on the photographs of the Civil War taken by Mathew B. Brady and his assistants:

_____ **a.** Brady's assistants took most Civil War photos; Brady almost blind

_____ **b.** History of development of photography

_____ **c.** Brady authorized to accompany Union troops and document war

_____ **d.** Brady quote about going to Bull Run battlefield: "A spirit in my feet said 'Go' and I went."

_____ **e.** Walt Whitman's poems about the Civil War

_____ **f.** Brady's portrait photographs of Abraham Lincoln

_____ **g.** Causes of the Civil War

## EXERCISE 2 — Evaluating Your Notes

Sort your note cards into piles according to their headings. Take time to read each card. Ask yourself these questions:

■ Can I read what I wrote on each card?

■ Does each card have a source number and a page number?

■ Is every card directly related to a heading or subheading on my working outline?

■ Do I have too little information for some headings?

■ Do I have too much information for some headings?

■ Does the information on the note card really fit the heading I have put it under? Do I need to move the card to a different heading, or maybe discard it entirely?

On the lines below or on a separate sheet of paper, write a brief progress report. Mention any problems you have discovered as you evaluated your notes and what work still needs to be done.

_____

_____

_____

_____

_____

_____

_____

_____

# Coherence

**Arrange the information in a way that readers will easily understand.**

A paper is coherent when it is orderly and makes sense. You have already thought about ordering your ideas (as you wrote your working outline). Now it is time to check and rethink your organization. Arrange and rearrange your stacks of note cards until you are satisfied that the information flows in a logical way.

The three most common ways of ordering information are chronological (used to narrate the order of events in time), spatial (used to describe a place or object), and by importance (used to explain or to persuade). Using order of importance, ideas and details can be arranged from most to least important or from least to most important. You do not have to force one of these types of organization onto your paper. Just concentrate on arranging ideas and details in the clearest, most natural and logical way.

Try explaining to a partner or small writing group why you have arranged the sections of your paper as you have, and ask for feedback. Do they think that the order of ideas and details makes sense?

## EXERCISE 3 · Ensuring Coherence

Check your stacks of note cards against your working outline. Ask yourself the following questions, and then write a brief progress report on any problems you have discovered and changes you plan to make.

- Now that I have sorted and evaluated my note cards, have I discovered any problems in my working outline? If so, how do I propose to fix these problems?

- What feedback have I received from a partner or writing group? What changes, if any, do I plan to make in response to this feedback?

_____

_____

_____

_____

_____

_____

_____

_____

_____

_____

_____

_____

_____

# Audience and Purpose

**Identify your audience and your purpose.**

**Audience.** The manner in which you express your thesis statement and the way that you focus your paper depend in part on your intended audience. Imagine how a paper on the latest techniques for growing orchids might be tailored for each of the following audiences:

- members of an orchid club
- a group of middle-school students
- a group of senior citizens who have had no gardening experience
- a group of biology teachers

Audiences vary in what they need to know and want to know. Some of the audiences mentioned would know a lot about growing orchids; some would know nothing. For audiences that know little, you would have to define terms and provide background information. For those who already know a lot about orchids and other plants, you could skip the background and discuss technical details.

Clearly, the primary audience for your research paper is your teacher and your classmates. But can you find a special audience, too? If you are writing about legislation and advertising designed to prevent teenagers from smoking cigarettes, for instance, you might make your paper available to the school's science club or to a local group of advertising professionals.

**Purpose.** If you have not already decided on the purpose of your research paper, now is the time to pin it down. Your purpose will affect which details you choose to include and the way you express your ideas. Are you trying to persuade or explain? Are you comparing and contrasting, analyzing causes and effects, or proposing a solution to a problem? Perhaps your purpose is to interpret or evaluate a literary work or works? Whatever your purpose, you will better maintain the focus of your paper if you always keep in mind how you are trying to affect your audience.

**EXERCISE** **Identifying Your Audience and Purpose**

Stop to think about your research paper's audience and purpose. Answer each of the following questions in a complete sentence.

**1.** Who is the audience for my research paper?

_____

_____

**2.** What does my audience already know about the topic I am writing about? What might they need to know or want to know?

_____

_____

**3.** What other groups of people might be interested in this topic? How can I arrange to share my paper with them?

_____

_____

**4.** What is the purpose of my paper? (If possible, use one of the purposes mentioned on the preceding page—"analyze," "interpret," "explain," etc.)

_____

_____

# Thesis Statement

 **Draft a working thesis statement that tells what you will cover in your paper.**

A thesis statement is a single declarative sentence that states the controlling idea of your research paper. It identifies both your topic and your limited focus and suggests what the body of your paper will cover. Usually, the thesis statement is either the first or last sentence in the introductory paragraph.

## GUIDELINES

- A thesis statement is a single declarative sentence. It should not be expressed as a question. If you have phrased your limited topic as a research question, your thesis statement provides a one-sentence answer to that question.
- A thesis statement is a preview of what the paper is about. It states the topic and the writer's specific focus on the topic. (Do not begin with "The purpose of my paper is . . . ." or "In this paper, I will write about . . . .")
- A thesis statement controls the paper's content. Everything in the paper provides support for the thesis statement.
- A thesis statement may suggest, but should not state, your conclusions. Save your conclusions for the end of your paper.
- A thesis statement should have a confident tone. Sound as if you are sure of what you're saying. Avoid using "hedge" words and phrases, such as _probably, might, I think, seems, apparently, it seems to me_, etc.

 **EXERCISE** **Revising Thesis Statements**

Read each of the faulty thesis statements that follow. Revise each thesis statement so that it meets the requirements stated in the guidelines above. You may make up details if you wish.

**1.** The purpose of my paper is to write about how strikes in sports have affected fans.

_____

_____

_____

**2.** It seems to me that E-mail (electronic mail) is probably a very important thing in business and in personal communication.

_____

_____

_____

**3.** How does the amount and kind of television that teenagers watch influence their achievements in school?

_____

_____

_____

**4.** The purpose of my paper is to write about some of the many young-adult novels that deal with important issues that are helpful to their readers, who most likely never see counselors.

_____

_____

 **Here are several examples of faulty thesis statements. Note how each has been revised and improved.**

**WORDY AND TENTATIVE**
It seems to me that probably one of the seriously important decisions almost all teenagers face today is deciding what jobs they might have sometime in the future.

**CONFIDENT**
The most important dilemma today's teenagers face is making informed career decisions: choosing a type of work that will sustain them and preparing adequately for that career.

**VAGUE**
In this community crime is a problem that people can work together to overcome.

**SPECIFIC**
Crime Watch, a community-based resident patrol, is a practical, effective way for citizens of all ages to cooperate in protecting themselves and their community from crime.

**STATES TOPIC BUT DOES NOT LIMIT FOCUS**
Dogs can be trained to help disabled people.

**STATES TOPIC AND LIMITS FOCUS**
For thousands of disabled Americans, "service dogs" improve the emotional, social, and economic quality of life.

**QUESTION**
How can high-school students start a school radio station?

**STATEMENT**
With as little as $500, high-school students can create and staff a "drive-by" radio station, benefiting both the students and the school in significant ways.

## EXERCISE 6 · Drafting a Thesis Statement for Your Paper

Before you do this exercise, review your working outline and your stacks of note cards. Make sure you have a clear sense of the scope of your paper. Then write at least three significantly different versions of a thesis statement for your research paper. (Use a separate sheet of paper, if necessary.) Choose the thesis statement you like best. Share all of your thesis statements with a partner or writing group, and see if their preferences match yours. Try to express why the one you have chosen is the best.

_____

_____

_____

_____

_____

_____

_____

_____

_____

_____

_____

_____

_____

_____

_____

_____

_____

_____

_____

_____

_____

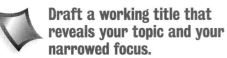

## Writing a Title

**Draft a working title that reveals your topic and your narrowed focus.**

Your title is the first chance you have to communicate your topic and your focus (the limited part of the topic you're tackling) to your reader. A good title should mention both:

Although you are far from having to finalize your title, a working title and thesis statement will help clarify your thinking and keep you on track as you prepare your final outline (Step 5) and write the first draft for your paper (Step 6).

**Title = Topic + Your Narrowed Focus**

**Here are some examples of faulty titles. Note how each has been revised and improved.**

**TOO VAGUE**
Credit Card Problems

**SPECIFIC**
Using Credit Cards: How to Keep from Going Under

---

**STATEMENT**
Too Many Children Don't Know What to Do in a Fire

**REVISED**
Teaching Children What to Do in a Fire

---

**TOO GENERAL**
Mystery Novels and Movies

**SPECIFIC**
Making a Mystery Novel into a Movie: Successes and Failures

---

**UNCLEAR**
Feeding the Diet Industry

**CLEAR**
The Diet Industry in America: Big Bucks

---

**TOO CUTE**
Escaping with the Wizard of Oz

**STRAIGHTFORWARD**
Ballooning as a Sport: Advantages and Disadvantages

---

**EXERCISE 7 Revising Titles**

This exercise will give you some practice before you tackle your own title. Clearly, it is difficult to write a good title for a paper you know nothing about. But see what you can do with these titles. Make up whatever you need (usually a focus) to improve the title. Then get together with a small group to compare and discuss your revisions.

**1.** The United Nations

_____

_____

**2.** Creativity Should Be Encouraged

_____

_____

**3.** TV's Greatest Hits

_____

_____

**4.** Special Effects

_____

_____

**5.** Edgar Allan Poe

_____

_____

**6.** Diets for Staying Alive

_____

_____

**7.** Teenagers and Cars

_____

_____

**8.** Popular Music

_____

_____

## Drafting a Title for Your Research Paper

On the lines below, write some titles (at least four) for your paper. Discuss them with a partner or writing group. Choose the one you like best. This can be your working title, and you can change it up until the day you turn your paper in.

# Computer Connection

If you have taken your notes on a computer, you should also have printed out a hard copy to work with. You can probably space out your computer notes so that three "note cards" fit on a page. Experiment until you get the spacing right. Then print all of your notes, and cut each one to note-card size so that you can sort them into stacks having the same heading. You may end up with some combination of handwritten note cards and computer-printed notes. No problem. But there is still nothing like handling physical pieces of paper or note cards when you are trying to organize and evaluate your notes.

## CHECKLIST REVIEW

☑ Sort your note cards into stacks having the same heading.

☑ Evaluate your notes.

☑ Make sure that all of the information fits the scope of your paper.

☑ Arrange the information in an order that readers can easily understand.

☑ Identify your audience and your purpose.

☑ Draft a working thesis statement that tells what you will cover in your paper.

☑ Draft a working title that reveals your topic and your narrowed focus.

# Write a Final Outline

Reprinted by permission: Tribune Media Services

**T**he last step before you actually start writing your paper is finalizing your outline. If you did a working outline in Step 3, you will need to update and revise it now. But the writing process isn't exactly the same for everyone. You may be a writer who writes first and outlines later. Check with your teacher to see if it's okay to postpone the outline step—not omit it altogether—until after you write your first draft. Keep in mind also that some teachers do not require a formal outline. Ask your teacher whether you will be asked to submit one.

## Content and Organization

Your final outline shows at a glance the two essential aspects of your paper: its content and its organization. Usually, a final outline includes a third element, your thesis statement, which comes right after the title and before the outline of the body of the paper.

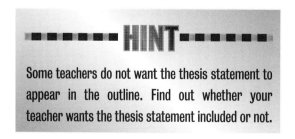

**HINT**

Some teachers do not want the thesis statement to appear in the outline. Find out whether your teacher wants the thesis statement included or not.

The three important parts of a research paper that *never* appear in an outline are the introductory paragraph(s), the paper's conclusion

or concluding paragraph(s), and the Works Cited list. You will learn more about these parts of your paper in Step 6 and Step 7.

 **Choose either a topic outline or a sentence outline.**

Your outline must be either a topic outline or a sentence outline—not a combination of both. You cannot mix the two types of outlines. Your teacher may make the decision for you by specifying which type you will be required to write.

In a topic outline, the headings and subheadings are a series of words or phrases, not complete sentences.

**Here is an example of a topic outline.**

I. Native American "code talkers" during World Wars I and II

    A. Who they were

        1. Their tribes

        2. Their languages

    B. What they did

    C. Why they were so successful

        1. Spoken (not written) languages

        2. Languages totally unfamiliar to enemy code breakers

In a sentence outline, every heading and subheading is a complete sentence. (A complete sentence contains a subject and a verb and expresses a complete thought.)

 **Here is an example of a sentence outline.**

I. Native Americans served successfully as "code talkers" in the United States Armed Forces during World Wars I and II.

    A. They were fluent speakers of their native languages.

        1. They were Choctaws, Navajos, Comanches, Winnebagos, Kiowas, and Cherokees.

        2. Each tribe spoke a unique language.

    B. Code talkers transmitted military information via walkie-talkie radios and field telephones to other speakers of their language.

    C. Enemy code breakers were unable to understand the Indians' languages.

        1. Almost all were spoken languages only and had no written form.

        2. These tribal languages were totally unfamiliar to outsiders.

---

## ■■■■■■■■■■■■■■■ HINT ■■■■■■■■■■■■■■

Each type of outline has its advantages. A topic outline is quicker and easier to write. Sentence outlines take more time but have two distinct points in their favor: (1) They furnish ready-made topic sentences for your paragraphs. (2) Because they force you to summarize what you are going to say about each topic, they can reveal problems in the organization of your ideas.

# The Form and Logic of an Outline

 **Follow the correct outline form.**
The main headings and subheadings are written in a standard form.

■ A number or letter precedes each heading. Each number or letter is followed by a period or is enclosed in parentheses.

■ The first word in every heading begins with a capital letter. Sentence outlines (but *not* topic outlines) have a period at the end of each heading.

■ Indentations show a heading's level of importance. An indented heading is a subdivision of the preceding heading.

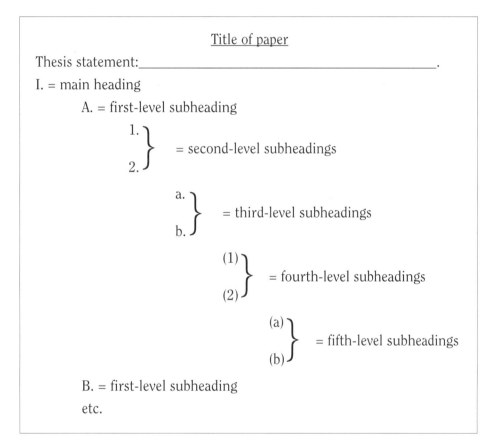

Title of paper

Thesis statement:_____.

I. = main heading

    A. = first-level subheading

        1.
        } = second-level subheadings
        2.

          a.
          } = third-level subheadings
          b.

            (1)
            } = fourth-level subheadings
            (2)

              (a)
              } = fifth-level subheadings
              (b)

    B. = first-level subheading

    etc.

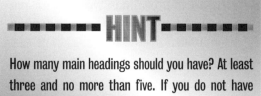 **Identify the major sections of your paper. These will be your main (Roman numeral) headings.**

How can you figure out what the main headings of your outline should be? If you did a working outline to help guide your note taking (Step 3), you have already made a stab at identifying the main headings and subheadings. Compare your stacks of note cards (separated according to headings) with your working outline: Do you want to change some of the main headings, or

reword them? Do you want to add new main headings? Do you want to drop some of the main headings?

**HINT**

How many main headings should you have? At least three and no more than five. If you do not have enough main headings, or if you have too many, rethink the organization of your paper.

When you are figuring out your main headings and subheadings, you are using the critical-thinking skill of **analysis**: You are breaking your topic into its smaller, separate parts. (When you analyze something, you break it into its separate parts and examine each part separately. You analyze a short story, for instance, by discussing its plot, characters, point of view, setting, and theme.)

Throughout your outline, make sure that headings and subheadings are **discrete**—that is, entirely separate. Headings and subheadings should not overlap or duplicate each other. There are two things wrong with the main headings in the following example. Can you find them both?

ILLOGICAL

> *Topic*: Why the movie *The Wizard of Oz* remains an enduring classic

> I. Its plot
> II. Its story line
> III. Its music
> IV. Its visual effects and songs

Main headings I and II are about the same thing (plot and story line mean the same thing), and the "songs" part of heading IV duplicates the "music" of heading III.

LOGICAL

> *Topic*: Why the movie *The Wizard of Oz* remains an enduring classic

> I. Its plot
> II. Its characters
> III. Its music
> IV. Its special effects

Here are four common types of research papers with examples of how the topic has been broken up into main headings.

**1. Examine a problem. Discuss one or more solutions.**

> *Topic*: How to reduce school violence

> I. Statistics past and present
> II. Solution 1: school crime-watch organization
> III. Solution 2: peer mediation program
> IV. Solution 3: increased security

**2. Examine an effect. Discuss several causes.**

> *Topic*: What has caused the greenhouse effect, and how serious is it?

> I. Increased burning of fossil fuels (coal, gas, oil) produces increase in carbon dioxide and other greenhouse gases.
> II. Even small environmental changes may lead to significant global warming.
> III. Clouds may either raise or lower Earth's temperatures.

**3. Examine a cause. Discuss several effects.**

> *Topic*: Beneficial effects of regular exercise and a low-fat diet

> I. Decrease in heart disease
> II. Decrease in obesity
> III. Increase in average life span

**4. History of something (a movement, an event, an idea)**

> *Topic*: The essay, a relatively new literary form

> I. First *Essays* (French lawyer Michel de Montaigne, 1533-1592)
> II. Formal essays (e.g., Ralph Waldo Emerson, 1803-1882)
> III. Informal essays (20th century)

# EXERCISE 1 — Analyzing a Topic to Formulate Main Headings

Use your imagination and common sense to write three or four main headings that might be covered in a research paper on each of the numbered topics. (NOTE: There are no "right" answers to this exercise—only different approaches to analyzing the topic.) Work with a partner or in a small group and compare your main headings with those of your classmates.

1. How to increase voter turnout in the United States

    I._____

    II._____

    III._____

    IV._____

2. Automobiles powered by electric batteries

    I._____

    II._____

    III._____

    IV._____

3. The three (or four) best things about television

    I._____

    II._____

    III._____

    IV._____

4. How advertisers persuade you to buy their products

    I._____

    II._____

    III._____

    IV._____

# EXERCISE 2 — Identifying the Main Headings in Your Research Paper

Write your topic and the working title of your research paper. On the lines below, divide your paper into at least three main headings.

Topic _____

Working Title _____

I. _____

II._____

III._____

IV._____

V._____

**Divide the main headings into subheadings and then into sub-subheadings, as needed. You can never have only one sub-heading; you must have at least two.**

It is not logical to divide a larger heading into only one subheading. (Think of dividing a whole pie into pieces: You can cut the pie many different ways, but you must have at least two pieces—or you have not divided the pie.)

Here is part of an outline showing subheadings and sub-subheadings:

*Topic*: Why the movie *The Wizard of Oz* remains an enduring classic

I. Its plot

   A. Frame of story

      1. Tornado in Kansas

      2. Return to Kansas

   B. Fantastic adventure

   C. Suspenseful conflicts

      1. Good vs. evil

      2. Struggle to return home

II. Its characters

   A. Girl as hero

   B. Sympathetic scarecrow, tin man, lion

## Computer Connection

Most word-processing programs have a built-in outline capability. Check the index in the program's manual to find instructions on how to create a formal (traditional) outline. Some word-processing programs have Outline View as an option in the View menu. Outline View enables you to indent paragraphs in the draft of your paper to show how ideas are related.

**Within any level, word the headings so they are parallel in structure.**

In writing, "parallel" means having the same grammatical structure. In the following excerpt, the headings in A, B, and C are parallel. Each heading is made up of a noun followed by an infinitive phrase ("to" plus a verb).

II. Instruments to predict volcanic eruptions

   A. Chemical sensor to analyze gases in volcanic plume

   B. Seismometer (buried sensor) to record vibrations in magma

   C. Sensors to measure cracks in volcano's surface

In the following example, the A, B, and C headings are not parallel.

II. Instruments to predict volcanic eruptions

    A. Chemical sensor for measuring gases in volcanic plume

    B. How a seismometer (buried sensor) is used

    C. Cracks on surface

Try this "bottom-up" technique to check the logic of your outline: Read the outline from the bottom up. Each group of lesser subheadings should "add up" to the more important heading above it.

**EXERCISE 3 — Parallel Structure**

Revise the following headings to make them parallel. Compare your revised headings with a partner's.

**1.** *Topic:* Jane Addams and her work

    I.   About Jane Addams' life

    II.  1889, helped found Hull House, a settlement house in Chicago.

    III. Addams had other interests.

        A. Her work for women's rights

        B. Winning the Nobel Peace Prize

**2.** *Topic:* Animated cartoons: the technology

    I.   Artists who draw cartoons by hand

        A. Summary of what makes cartoon characters move

        B. Earliest short cartoons

        C. In Walt Disney studios, the famous group of animators—the Nine Old Men—who created full-length movies such as *Bambi, Peter Pan, 101 Dalmatians*.

    II.  Animation done by computers

        A. How it works

        B. *Tron* (1984), first computer-animated film

    III. What is the future of animated cartoons?

## GUIDELINES TO MAKING AN OUTLINE

1. Write either a sentence outline or a topic outline. *Don't mix the two types.*

2. A number or letter precedes each heading. Each number or letter is followed by a period or enclosed in parentheses.

3. Every heading begins with a capital letter. Sentence outlines (but not topic outlines) have a period at the end of each heading.

4. Indentations show a heading's level of importance. An indented heading is a subdivision of the preceding heading.

5. If any heading calls for subheadings, there must be two or more.

6. The wording of headings within a section must be parallel.

**EXERCISE** **What Might the Headings Be?**

The following notes are for a report on the development of skyscrapers and their effects on the people who live and work in them. After you read the notes carefully, develop an outline based on them. (Use a separate sheet of paper, if necessary.) Keep in mind that there is no one "correct" way to outline these notes or those for any other topic. Try to make your headings and subheadings logical and parallel. Meet with several classmates to talk about your outlines based on these notes.

Thesis statement: Two American inventions—steel-frame construction and a safety device for elevators—led to the skyscraper, which altered earth's human landscape.

History of skyscrapers—Chicago

Before skyscrapers, masonry (brick or stone) construction—thick walls at base to support upper stories

Chicago fire Oct.8-10, 1871, destroyed 3 1/2 mi. central city → building boom

Steel-frame construction (in contrast to masonry) allowed windows, more room @ base, greater number of stories

1st skyscraper = 9-story Chicago's Home Insurance Co. Bldg. 1884-85, architect Major Wm. LeBaron Jenney, "father of the skyscraper"

Anecdote: Jenney got steel-frame construction idea when wife put heavy book on top of metal birdcage—thin wires supported it

Great Chicago architect—Louis Henry Sullivan. pp. 539-541

Importance of Elevator

Essential invention—elevators, "vertical railways"

In NYC, Elisha Graves Otis (1811-1861) invented safety device: stopped elevator from falling if chain broke; 1st passenger elevator 1857

Otis patented device in 1861, built steam elevators

"vertical railways"—used esp. in hotels; later powered by electric motors

pp. 537-538

[Notes from The Creators: A History of Heroes of the Imagination by Daniel J. Boorstin © 1992, New York: Random House]

History of word "skyscraper"

1794—triangular sail on a clipper ship; original meaning

1826—high-standing horse

1857—very tall man

1892—person riding a high cycle

1891—tall building of many stories; first use in Boston Massachusetts Journal

[from The Oxford English Dictionary, London: Oxford UP, 1933]

Effects of skyscrapers

Residential and business skyscrapers: treat separately?

Some effects: growth of cities as centers of commerce, greater population density, less human scale (no neighbors, no sense of community)

Positive: great views, lots of light, efficient use of city's limited space

Negative: "too impersonal," hate waiting for elevators

What Lewis Mumford says

"If fast transportation made the horizon the limit for urban sprawl, the new methods of construction made the 'sky the limit,' as gamblers loved to say."

Acc. to Mumford, urban density "befouled & poisonous air, constricted housing, demoralized social life, teeming with violence & crime"

[pp. 430-431, The City in History by Lewis Mumford, New York: Harcourt, Brace & World, 1961]

What workers say

Survey of people who work in skyscrapers

Their fears (safety: dependence on elevators & electricity; dangerous in earthquake & fire; target of terrorists)

Convenient to fast public transportation

[interview with neighbors, New Rochelle, New York, January 25, 1997]

_____

_____

_____

_____

_____

_____

_____

_____

_____

_____

_____

_____

_____

_____

_____

_____

_____

_____

_____

_____

_____

_____

_____

_____

_____

## Revising Your Working Outline

**EXERCISE**

Spend some time looking over your note cards and your working outline. Decide what changes you will need to make in your outline, and answer each of the questions below.

- ■ Which headings or subheadings need more information?
- ■ Are there headings or subheadings that need to be added?
- ■ Are there headings or subheadings that should be dropped?
- ■ Which headings or subheadings need to be changed or reworded?
- ■ What other changes do I need to make?

**EXERCISE 6**

## Writing Your Final Outline

On the lines below, write your final outline. Use a separate sheet of paper if you need more room.

_____

_____

_____

_____

_____

_____

_____

_____

_____

_____

_____

_____

_____

_____

_____

_____

_____

_____

_____

_____

_____

_____

_____

_____

_____

_____

_____

_____

_____

_____

_____

_____

_____

_____

_____
_____
_____
_____
_____
_____
_____
_____
_____
_____
_____
_____
_____
_____
_____
_____
_____
_____
_____
_____
_____
_____
_____
_____

## CHECKLIST REVIEW

☑ Choose either a topic outline or a sentence outline.

☑ Follow the correct outline form.

☑ Identify the major sections of your paper. These will be your main (Roman numeral) headings.

☑ Divide the main headings into subheadings and smaller subheadings, as needed. You can never have only one sub-heading; you must have at least two.

☑ Within any level, word the headings so they are parallel in structure.

# Write the First Draft

*Y*ou have passed the halfway mark in
the writing of your research paper.
*You have your note cards and*
*(probably) a final outline. You have*
*drafted a thesis statement and a*
*working title. Now you need to pull it all*
*together in sentences and paragraphs.*
*You will use the critical-thinking skill*
*called* **synthesis**. *Synthesis is the*
*putting together of all kinds of pieces*
*and parts and creating something new.*
*A research paper in a way is a big*
*synthesis. You start out with lots of raw*
*material—notes about other people's*

*"Period. New paragraph."*

Drawing by Carl Rose; © 1950 The New Yorker Magazine, Inc.

*ideas—and you end up with something unique: a paper that is*
*different from anything that anybody has ever written before.*

## What You Do Not Have to Do

Let's start with five things you *don't* have to
do when you draft your paper:

**1.** You don't absolutely *have to* have a final
outline before you start drafting. You may
be one of those write-first, outline-later
writers who asks, "How do I know what
I'm going to write until I see what I've
written?"

**2.** You don't have to write the introduction,
body, and conclusion in that order. Some
people write from the beginning to the
end of the paper. Other writers—with
equally good results—draft the body first
and leave the introduction and conclusion until last.

**3.** You don't have to write the body of your
paper in the order shown in your outline.

Just start somewhere with the main idea
that you feel most confident about. Draft
that whole Roman numeral section. Then
pick another section to attack.

**4.** You do not have to think about niceties.
You need not worry too much about writing perfectly formed sentences at this
step. You will have plenty of time for all
that later when you revise (Step 8). For
the moment just focus on getting your
ideas onto paper (or a computer screen).

**5.** You don't have to panic. If you discover
that something is lacking or otherwise
amiss, it is not too late to fix it. There is
still time to do more research to plug a
hole or to refocus your thesis statement
or to make other adjustments.

## SOME GENERAL GUIDELINES FOR DRAFTING YOUR PAPER

Since the writing process is different for everyone, there is no lockstep list of rules you must follow as you draft your paper. You may follow the suggestions here, or you may do it your own way. Just make sure that you do not put off drafting and that you leave yourself plenty of time to do a good job later on when it comes time to revise and put your paper in final form.

1. Your first draft is a big start but it is just a beginning. Remember, nothing is chiseled in stone. You will make lots of changes (see Step 8) before you are done.

2. Try to write your first draft in one sitting, without interruption. Find a quiet place and stay focused until you have finished. If you cannot finish in one sitting, try to do it in two or three sessions.

3. Follow your outline, but adjust it as needed. If something just doesn't work, drop it. If something needs to be put in, add it.

4. Write in the third-person point of view. (Do not mention yourself; do not use the pronouns *I* or *me* or *we*). This will give your paper an objective, factual tone.

5. Find your own voice. Express your ideas as clearly and directly as you can. Do not use fancy-sounding words that you cannot define.

6. Give credit! Do not pass off anyone else's words or ideas as your own. Keep very careful track of your sources, and be sure to document them.

7. Save everything. Do not trash any of your note cards or—if you have taken notes on a computer—note card documents.

## Computer Connection

Have you written papers or letters on a computer before? If you are used to writing on a computer, you know how easy it is to write and revise. If you are still writing longhand first, then keyboarding what you have written, that is fine, too. But you might want to try composing directly on a computer, especially if you have never tried it. Be sure to save your work at regular intervals (every 5 minutes or so if the computer does not do it for you automatically) so that you do not risk losing what you have written if there is a power failure or a computer malfunction. Print your draft periodically as you write, so you can read the whole text and judge how well the ideas hang together.

# Writing an Introduction

**Write an introduction that *attracts your reader's attention* and clearly indicates what your paper will be about. Include your thesis statement somewhere in your introduction.**

For a long research paper, your introduction may take one paragraph or several. Often, the thesis statement is the first or last sentence of the introduction. It points the way toward the body of your paper, indicating the main ideas you will cover there. Your introduction should also provide background information and define any key terms that readers need to know.

There is no single "correct" way to introduce your topic. You could probably write five or six distinct and equally effective introductions. In fact, it is a good idea to draft several entirely different approaches and choose the one you like best. Here are some tried-and-true ways that you might consider (but if you come up with something better, by all means go for it).

- Tell a brief story (an anecdote).
- Describe a problem or condition.
- Ask a question.
- Cite some startling or interesting fact or statistics.
- Quote a powerful or intriguing idea.

Three things you should *not* do in your introduction: (1) Don't try to be funny. (2) Don't repeat the title. (3) Don't state your purpose: "The purpose of this paper is..."

In Step 10, you'll find a model research paper entitled "The Cuban Missile Crisis: Immediate Responses and Lasting Effects." The writer begins her paper with an interesting fact about a character (symbol) in Chinese writing. Although that fact seems totally unrelated to her topic, she uses it to capture the reader's attention and also to make a comparison. The writer's thesis statement is set in boldface type.

     The Chinese character for the word "crisis" has two very different meanings. The first is the meaning we usually associate with the word in English: "a dangerous event or period." But the same character can also mean "opportunity." The fact that a crisis can actually have beneficial effects or can be the means for reaching a new understanding is often overlooked in international politics (Craig and George 129). The Soviets call it the Caribbean Crisis; the Cubans call it the October Crisis; to the rest of the world it is the Cuban Missile Crisis (Finkelstein 103-04). It is a crisis that brought the United States and the Soviet Union into their first direct confrontation of the nuclear age and drew the world to the very brink of nuclear destruction. **By looking at the press coverage of the Cuban**

Missile Crisis at the time that it was happening, we can better understand the responses of Americans who lived through the crisis and how it changed their views. From our later perspective, we can also see that the crisis had important effects in both national and world politics.

## Computer Connection

If you have written notes on a computer, copy them into the document that you are using for your first draft. You can "copy and paste" quotations and other ideas where they belong in your draft (in the appropriate paragraph). Then you can reword them or incorporate them into your own sentences.

**EXERCISE 1** **Analyzing an Introduction**

Read the following introduction and answer each question. Meet with a partner or small group to talk about your answers.

> At first glance, it is difficult to see any similarities between Alice's adventures in Wonderland and those of the central character in Hermann Hesse's Siddhartha. Alice's adventures are those of a young girl in a world of imagination and nonsense. Siddhartha tells of the quest of an Indian boy for spiritual fulfillment. However, when we look at the underlying messages in these books, it becomes clear that what the main characters experience is very much alike. Their journeys, so different on the surface, merge into one path. The similarities of Alice's and Siddhartha's adventures can be shown through examination of the characters, their situations, and the novels' symbols.

**1.** From this introduction, can you identify the three main sections (Roman numeral headings) of the research paper? What do you think they are?

_____

_____

_____

_____

**2.** What, if anything, do you think the writer might do to improve this introduction?

_____

_____

_____

_____

_____

 **EXERCISE**

## Writing an Introduction

Draft a one- or two-paragraph introduction based on the notes that follow. You may make up any details you need. Read aloud and then discuss your introduction with a group of classmates.

> Kids with Reading Problems
> Ways to teach young children alphabet & sounds of letters; 4 different types of learning w. suggestions for activities:
> 1. visual—look for food labels, make collage of newspaper letters
> 2. auditory (hearing)—make up song, sentences w. words begin. w. sound
> 3. tactile (touch)—finger-paint letters; use glue & macaroni, sand, sparkles to make letter shapes
> 4. kinesthetic (motion)—outline letter w. chalk & have kid walk the letter
>
> pp. 130-135, Solving Your Child's Reading Problems ©1993 by Ricki Linksman (Director of National Reading Diagnostics Institute), New York: Carol Publishing Group

_____

_____

_____

_____

_____

_____

_____

_____

_____

_____

_____

_____

_____

**EXERCISE 3** **Drafting Your Introduction**

On a separate piece of paper, draft two or three entirely different introductions for your research paper. Share these introductions with a small group of classmates and ask for feedback. Decide on the introduction you like best.

## Writing the Body of Your Paper

 **Keep very careful track of your sources. Insert your bibliography source card number after ideas or quotations that need to be acknowledged.**

This is the point where documenting sources can go awry and the possibility of accidental plagiarism occurs. Keep watch on your note cards for those large quotation marks that alert you to a direct quotation. Pay careful attention to ideas that need documenting, too. Plug in parentheses and source card numbers at the appropriate spots. (You will learn all the ins and outs of **parenthetical citation** in the next chapter, Step 7.)

 **Write in the present tense. Use the past tense only to refer to historical events.**

This advice about tenses follows the MLA (Modern Language Association) style, which is preferred by most high-school teachers. Even though a work of literature was written long ago, the work still exists, so the present tense is used to discuss the work.

> **Here are some examples showing correct use of present and past tense according to MLA style.**

PRESENT TENSE — In "I heard a Fly buzz—when I died—" Emily Dickinson **describes** what the speaker in the poem **feels** at the moment of death.

PRESENT TENSE — In his *Philosophiae naturalis principia mathematica* (1687), Sir Isaac Newton **describes** his laws of universal gravity.

PAST TENSE — In 1901, Beatrix Potter **published** *The Tale of Peter Rabbit* privately.

PAST TENSE — Sir Isaac Newton **built** a reflecting telescope in 1668.

**APA Style** The APA (American Psychological Association) is the style used in college and professional papers in the social sciences. A similar style is used in the sciences and in business. According to the APA style (see Appendix B), the past tense or past perfect tense is used to describe a scientist's or writer's work that was completed in the past. Follow your teacher's directions on which of these styles to follow.

PAST TENSE — In his *Philosophiae naturalis principia mathematica* (1687), Sir Isaac Newton **described** his laws of universal gravity.

**Each paragraph in the body should state a main idea in a topic sentence. The rest of the sentences in that paragraph should provide supporting details.**

Topic sentences perform two useful functions in informative, or expository, writing—the kind of writing you are doing in a research paper. A **topic sentence** states the paragraph's main idea and also controls the paragraph's content. All of the other sentences in the paragraph should support the topic sentence, offering convincing evidence or proof. Try to provide information from at least two different sources to support each topic sentence.

In the two paragraphs that follow, the topic sentences are boldfaced. Notice that in the first paragraph, Andrea Wang, a high school student in Garden City, New York, uses two sentences—a question and an answer—as the topic sentence.

> **What is causing the destruction of rain forests? The answer is human exploitation.** According to the Food and Agriculture Organization of the United Nations (FAO), about 250 million farmers live in rain forests around the world. They occupy forest areas owned by the state, in search of land for crop-growing and livestock-raising. Very often, the state cannot control access to these forest areas. Some of the farmers, who are new to the rain forest, follow the roads and trails made by the loggers and, mainly by using fire, they create "frontiers," which push back the forest. Crops are greedy eaters of forest. In Ethiopia, big plantations have replaced trees: 60 percent of the land is now used for cotton growing and 22 percent for sugarcane. In Central America, two-thirds of the forests have been sacrificed for livestock-raising.
>
> **Another factor in deforestation is the timber industry.** Suriname had been 90 percent covered by virgin rain forest until 1993, when the government granted 150,000 hectares (one hectare equals 2.47 acres) to an Indonesian logging company. The problem with logging is that even if one tree needs to be cut down, other trees around it are harmed and trails have to be cut. This opens the way to land-hungry farmers, according to "Conserving Wildlife in Tropical Forests Managed for Timber" by Peter Frumhoff in the July/August '95 edition of BioScience.

## EXERCISE 4  What's Wrong with This Paragraph?

Get together with a partner to talk about this paragraph from the body of a research paper.

> Many primates have been trained to perform as humans do. I've seen them often, in circuses, in shows, and in movies. You probably have, too. Three out of every five chimpanzees can be trained, while two out of every five orangutans can. Without too much labor and a great deal of difficulty, orangs can sit at a table, eat and drink like humans, ride a tricycle or bicycle, dress themselves, open a lock with a key and even pick the right key out of a half dozen or more, and pound nails with a hammer. One orang learned how to pedal and ride a tricycle in only three lessons—much faster than a small child usually learns.

**1.** What do you think this research paper is about?

_____

_____

**2.** What is the topic sentence of this paragraph?

_____

_____

**3.** Does the paragraph provide enough support for its topic sentence? How many different kinds of support are given?

_____

_____

**4.** Tell why you do or do not believe the writer's facts and statistics. What is missing from this paragraph?

_____

_____

**EXERCISE** **Writing a Paragraph**

Use the information in the following note cards to write one paragraph for the body of a research paper. The title and thesis statement are given below. (On the note cards, the abbreviation Q. stands for Quetzalcoatl.)

Title: <u>The Legends of Quetzalcoatl and King Arthur</u>

Thesis statement: The ancient Mexican god Quetzalcoatl and the legendary English King Arthur are similar in startling ways.

---

Legend of Quetzalcoatl                                          3

Portrayed as plumed (feathered) serpent; the Toltec (pre-Aztec Mexican people) god who gave corn, learning, arts.

Q. also an actual ruler—sent into exile when high priests disgraced him, in conflict with sky god.

"Q. the ruler eventually became identified with the god, and his story is a mixture of history and legend."

Legend of his promise to return important to Aztecs, 16th c.: Exiled from Tula; made a raft of serpents & set off across sea; vowed to return to reclaim his throne in year called 1 Reed.

(My note: Something like King Arthur's leaving on a boat, vowing to return when Britain is in need. Is Q. like King Arthur? Compare & contrast them?)

pp. 19-20, 25   <u>Aztec Civilization</u>, in World History Series. Lois Warburton © 1995, San Diego: Lucent Books

---

Legend of Quetzalcoatl                                          5

Q's rivalry with Tezcatlipoca, war god. Q. = "Father and Creator, the source of agriculture, science, and the arts. He was an enlightened god, the morning star and the evening star."

Various versions of Q's death: sailed toward east on raft of serpents; parted Gulf of Mexico's waters & walked away; became morning star; smoke from funeral pyre; ➜ quetzal birds. All have in common: prophecy that one day he would return.

pp. 75-76, 500 Nations, Alvin M. Josephy, Jr., New York: Knopf, 1994; see <u>also 2-page mural</u> of Q's life, pp.62-63 by Mexican artist Diego Rivera

---

Legend of King Arthur                                                    6
Legendary Celtic warrior-king, 5th-6th c., who fought Saxons
Reigned at Camelot w. knights of Round Table (A. & his knights
represented "ideal of medieval knighthood and chivalry")
A. killed in battle, body borne away by boat to isle of Avalon;
prophecy of his return someday

pp.156-157, The Columbia Encyclopedia, 5th edition, NY: Columbia
UP, 1993

_____
_____
_____
_____
_____
_____
_____
_____
_____
_____
_____
_____
_____
_____
_____
_____

**EXERCISE** ## Writing the Body of Your Research Paper

Use separate sheets of paper (or a computer and printer) to draft the body
of your research paper. When you have finished, ask yourself these questions about your writing process.

■ How long did it take me to draft the body?  How many "sittings"?

■ How many pages did I write? Do I feel that the body of my paper is about
the right length? too short? too long?

■ In what order did I write the body of my paper? From beginning to end?
Skipping around?

■ Did I follow my final outline? (Did I work from an outline?) Do I need to
revise my outline?

■ Did I use all of my note cards? Which ones did I not use, and why?

- Did I write a topic sentence for every paragraph? Did I have adequate support for each topic sentence?
- How pleased am I with the draft of the body of my paper? What work still needs to be done?

## Writing the Conclusion

Here is a common mistake: You are so glad to be finished with the body of your paper that you lose momentum and concentration—and your paper ends with a thud. Avoid this mistake by spending just as much time working on your conclusion as you did on the introduction.

**Write a conclusion that brings your paper to a satisfying close and says something worthwhile.**

Instead of just rephrasing your thesis statement, see if you can leave the reader with something to think about. Try these approaches:

- Offer a judgment.
- Make a final comment or observation.
- End with a quotation that pulls it all together.
- Summarize your main idea(s).
- Refer to your introduction.

In this concluding paragraph, Andrea Wang mentions several possible solutions to the rain forest problem and offers a final comment—or judgment—about where responsibility for the solution ultimately lies.

The United Nations Environment Programme (UNEP), the World Bank, and the World Resources Institute (WRI) have been trying to achieve sustainable management of the rain forests in an ongoing process known as the Tropical Forestry Action Plan. **There are many solutions for preserving rain forests.** One is to limit the time period of concessions granted to logging companies and making their renewal dependent on "good behavior." Skid trails should also be made because, according to the "Green, Red Alert for the Earth's Green Belt" by Frances Bequette in UNESCO Courier, 15 to 30 percent of the damage to forests is caused by tractors foraging randomly in search of felled trees. Felling techniques could also be improved so that falling trees cause their neighbors less damage. Eventually, helicopters and blimps could lift timber vertically out of the forest, avoiding trails. **The preservation of the rain forest depends mainly on countries. Either countries tolerate tree-felling and impose taxes on it, or they define regulations for using and managing the forests.**

# EXERCISE 7 Analyzing a Conclusion

Here is a writer's conclusion for a research paper about the American poet Theodore Roethke. Read the conclusion and then answer the questions that follow.

> Theodore Roethke was a bold and brilliant poet, whose explanations of nature and his own soul gave us some of the best and most unusual poetry in American literary history. His poetry was greatly influenced by his early years and is perhaps all the more searing because it cost him so much inside—cost him, at times, his very sanity. However, as Robert Boyers says:
>
> > It is his triumph that his best poems permit us to embrace the principle of change as the root of stability; that his best poems, through rhythm and syntax and diction, so evoke passion that we are able actively to sympathize with his sense of loss; and that we can feel, with him, how all finite things reveal infinitude. (5)
>
> In all of these things, Roethke is truly unique. Theodore Roethke's poetry shows us the pattern of the universe by showing us the pattern on a leaf; he gives us a glimpse of himself, and in doing so gives us an unforgettable glimpse of ourselves and all of mankind.

**1.** From this conclusion can you identify the two main sections (Roman numeral headings) of the research paper? What do you think they are?

_____

_____

_____

_____

**2.** Do you think this conclusion would be better or worse without the long quotation from Robert Boyers? Explain why you think so.

_____

_____

**3.** What, if anything, do you think the writer could do to improve this conclusion?

_____

_____

## EXERCISE 8 — Writing a Conclusion for Your Research Paper

On a separate sheet of paper, write at least two different conclusions. Read them aloud to several classmates and ask for their feedback. Then decide on the one you think is best.

## Using Direct Quotations

Some of your note cards probably contain direct quotations that you think you might use in your paper. As you were taking notes, you enclosed them in large quotation marks just to make sure you would know they are not your own words, and you also checked them carefully for accuracy.

> **•••••••• HINT ••••••••**
>
> Do not use too many quotations (an overload gets boring), and keep them fairly brief. Also, do not keep quoting from a single source. Use a sprinkling of direct quotations from different sources.

 **Follow the conventions for using direct quotations. Make sure that you clearly identify the source of the quotation.**

In the examples that follow, the numbers in parentheses indicate the bibliographical source card number of the quote (and in poetry the line numbers also). These are temporary citations only. You will learn about **parenthetical citation** in Step 7.

### Prose Quotations

■ Run prose quotations into the text if they are four typed lines or shorter.

*At the beginning of a sentence:*

"You gain strength, courage and confidence by every experience in which you really stop to look fear in the face," Eleanor Roosevelt writes(14).

*At the end of a sentence:*

Eleanor Roosevelt, who was painfully shy as a young woman, might have been writing about herself when she declared, "You gain strength, courage and confidence by every experience in which you really stop to look fear in the face"(14).

*Interrupted quotation:*

"You gain strength, courage and confidence," Eleanor Roosevelt writes, "by every experience in which you really stop to look fear in the face"(14).

- You do not have to quote whole sentences. Enclose words or phrases in quotation marks and run them into your sentences.

```
Ernesto Gallarza describes both the diffi-
culties and kindnesses he experienced in the
course of "the Americanization of Mexican
me"(12).
```

- If a prose quotation is longer than four typed lines, set it off from the rest of the text. Start a new line and indent ten spaces from the left margin. Do not use quotation marks for these long quotes.

```
Jane Austen sets the tone and theme of her
comic novel Pride and Prejudice in its open-
ing sentences:
        It is a truth universally acknowledged,
        that a single man in possession of a good
        fortune must be in want of a wife.
        However little known the feelings or
        views of such a man may be on his first
        entering a neighborhood, this truth is so
        well fixed in the minds of the surround-
        ing families, that he is considered as
        the rightful property of someone or other
        of their daughters.(2)
```

## Quotations from Poems

- Run in three or fewer lines quoted from a poem and use a slash mark (/) to indicate the end of a line. Enclose the quoted lines in quotation marks. (The line numbers of the poem are shown in parentheses.)

```
Walt Whitman's "Song of Myself" begins with
these lines: "I celebrate myself, and sing
myself,/ And what I assume you shall assume,/
For every atom belonging to me as good
belongs to you" (4.1-3).
```

- When quoting more than three lines from a poem, write each line as it appears in the poem. Indent the quoted lines, and do not use quotation marks.

```
In "The Raven," his most famous poem, Edgar
Allan Poe bombards the reader with a whole
gamut of sound effects to produce a chilling,
hypnotic effect, as in this first stanza:
        Once upon a midnight dreary, while I
            pondered, weak and weary,
        Over many a quaint and curious volume
            of forgotten lore—
        While I nodded, nearly napping, suddenly
            there came a tapping,
```

```
   As of someone gently rapping, rapping at
      my chamber door.
   "'Tis some visitor," I muttered, "tapping
      at my chamber door—
         Only this and nothing more." (3.1-6)
```

### Ellipses and Brackets

■ Use an ellipsis (a series of three periods separated by spaces) to show where you have omitted words in a quotation. If the quotation comes at the end of a sentence, add a fourth period as end punctuation.

```
In his introduction to A Tale of Two Cities,
Shuckburgh compares Madame Defarge to Lady
Macbeth, calling the Defarges "among the
greatest—and most terrible—of Dickens's cre-
ations, perhaps of all ... fiction."
```

```
Charles Dickens begins A Tale of Two Cities
with a description of the year 1775: "It was
the best of times, it was the worst of times.
It was the age of wisdom, it was the age of
foolishness,..."
```

■ Use brackets to enclose words that you insert in a quotation in order to make the meaning clear.

```
U.S. Senator William Fulbright told the
Senate, "We are handicapped by [foreign]
policies based on old myths rather than cur-
rent realities" (12).
```

**EXERCISE** ## Using Quotations

On the lines provided, write sentences that incorporate all or part of each quotation. Punctuate each quotation correctly.

**1.** "I have a dream that one day this nation will rise up and live out the true meaning of its creed: 'We hold these truths to be self-evident: that all men are created equal.' "

   —Dr. Martin Luther King, Jr., August 28, 1963, at the March on Washington, DC

_____

_____

_____

_____

_____

_____

**2.** Polonius, Laertes's father, saying farewell to his son:

> "This above all: to thine own self be true,
> And it must follow, as the night the day,
> Thou canst not then be false to any man."

> —Act I, scene 3, line 75, *Hamlet* by William Shakespeare

_____

_____

_____

_____

_____

_____

**3.** "There are only two or three human stories, and they go on repeating themselves as fiercely as if they had never happened before."

> —Willa Cather (American novelist), in *O Pioneers!* Chapter 4, Part II [1913]

_____

_____

_____

## CHECKLIST REVIEW

☑ **Write an introduction that attracts your reader's attention and clearly indicates what your paper will be about.**

☑ **Keep very careful track of your sources.**

☑ **Write in the present tense. Use the past tense only to refer to historical events.**

☑ **Every paragraph in the body should deal with a main idea, which is stated in its topic sentence. The rest of the sentences in the paragraph should provide adequate supporting details.**

☑ **Follow the conventions for using direct quotations. Make sure that you clearly identify the source of the quotation.**

# Document Sources

PEANUTS reprinted by permission of United Feature Syndicate, Inc.

*In Step 6 you completed the first draft of your research paper. Let it sit for a time while you do two tasks (parenthetical citations and your Works Cited list) that are important but less taxing than writing. In fact, the next step—documenting your sources—is probably the easiest one of all. Check your progress against the timetable you have selected. Are you on schedule?*

## Parenthetical Citation

When you wrote the first draft, you carefully put your bibliography source card number in parentheses whenever you needed to give credit for a quote or an idea. This form of documentation was only temporary. Now it is time to do it the right way.

**Follow the style of documentation that your teacher specifies.**

Most teachers prefer the MLA style of parenthetical documentation, which is the style employed in this chapter. (See Appendix B for a discussion of APA style.)

Whenever you insert a parenthetical cita-tion, you have two things to decide:

- where to place the citation
- what information belongs inside the parentheses.

 **Give credit for every quotation and paraphrase.**

You will want to document accurately any words or ideas that you have bor-rowed, but it is not necessary to document common knowledge or every single sen-tence. Try not to overload your paper with citations. You can group ideas so that you cover a spread of pages in a single citation.

Here are some rules governing the placement and punctuation of citations:

- **Place a citation at a natural pause—at the end of a sentence or after a phrase or clause.**

  In fact, "the fate of man hinges on the will-ingness to communicate" ("Showdown").

According to the *MLA Handbook*, the end of a sentence is preferred. However, a parenthetical citation should always come near the quotation or paraphrase it documents, so it may naturally fall somewhere in the middle of a sentence.

> "A full-scale blockade generally has been interpreted as an act of war," the Miami Herald reported ("Blockade"), and everyone feared what might happen.

■ **Place a citation at the end of a text sentence before the end punctuation mark.**

> Fearing nuclear attack, people descended on supermarkets for canned foods, water, candles, and batteries (Grunwald).

■ **If a citation follows a quotation at the end of a sentence, place the citation after the final quotation marks and before the sentence's end punctuation.**

> "I'll not vote for him," a New York salesman commented after the blockade was announced, "but I'll support him. His reaction was long overdue" (Robertson).

■ **A citation in the middle of a sentence comes before a comma, a colon, or a semicolon.**

> "A full-scale blockade generally has been interpreted as an act of war," the Miami Herald reported ("Blockade"), and everyone feared what might happen.

■ **For a long quote set off from the rest of the text, place the citation on the last line of the quote following the end punctuation mark. Follow this style for both prose and poetry.**

> Finkelstein notes that there were secret government plans:
>
> > At the White House plans were finalized for an evacuation of key governmental personnel and their families if Washington came under nuclear attack. Special passes were distributed and an assembly area was designated at the Reno Reservoir in northwest Washington, where a motorcade would be formed to transport people to the relocation area....The president himself did not consider leaving Washington. (85)

The form of the citation varies depending on the source. Use the following guidelines.

*One Author*

■ **Enclose in parentheses the author's last name and the page number where the quotation or idea can be found. Do not use any punctuation between the name and page number. Write the page number only. Do not use the word *page* or *pages* or the abbreviation *p.* or *pp.***

```
The Soviets call it the Caribbean Crisis; the
Cubans call it the October Crisis; to the
rest of the world it is the Cuban Missile
Crisis (Finkelstein 103-04).
```

■ **If the author's name appears in the text, write only the page number in parentheses.**

```
Robert Kennedy, the President's brother and
attorney general, revealed that the withdraw-
al had been verified with the help of the UN
and aerial photographs (113).
```

■ **If you refer to a complete work, omit page numbers.**

```
In 1990, almost thirty years after the cri-
sis, the Government released a whole series
of documents directly related to the Cuban
Missile Crisis (National Security Archives).
```

*More than One Work by an Author*

■ **Follow the styles shown in these examples:**

```
Our first glimpse of the "metallic" Miss
Murdstone makes us fear for the young David
(Dickens, David Copperfield, ch.4).
```

```
"It is a far, far better thing that I do, than
I have ever done," says Sydney Carton at the
end of A Tale of Two Cities (Dickens ch.40).
```

*Two or More Authors*

■ **If there are two authors, cite both authors' last names. Do not include the word *edited* or the abbreviation *ed.* in the citation.**

```
The fact that a crisis can actually have bene-
ficial effects or can be the means for reach-
ing a new understanding is often overlooked in
international politics (Craig and George 129).
```

■ **If there are three or more authors, either cite every author's last name or use the first author's name followed by *et al.* ("and others"). Use the same style (authors' names or *et al.*) in your Works Cited list.**

```
In philosopher Karl Popper's "open society,"
everyone is free to criticize Government
without fear of punishment. It is the oppo-
site of a totalitarian society (Bullock,
Stallybrass, and Trombley 608).
```

```
In 1993, infectious diseases killed 16.5 mil-
lion people worldwide, more than three times
the number who died from cancer (Brown et al.
115).
```

*No Author*

■ **If no author is given, use a single key word to refer to the title (the word by which the work is alphabetized in the Works Cited list). Use quotation marks for the title of an article or editorial. Underline the title of a book.**

```
Newsweek summed it up: "Mr. Kennedy's behavior
during the past two weeks has given Americans
a sense of deep confidence in the temper of
their President" ("Lessons").
```

*Electronic Sources*

■ **For an Internet or CD-ROM source, cite the first word or first few words of the Works Cited list entry.**

```
On October 26, Khruschev sent a letter offering
to withdraw the missiles if the U.S. pledged
not to invade Cuba ("The Cuban Missile").
```

■ **Cite the writer of an E-mail message. If the Works Cited list has two works by the same person, specify the E-mail message.**

```
Fearing nuclear attack, people descended on
supermarkets for canned foods, water, candles,
and batteries (Grunwald, E-mail).
```

━━━━━━ **HINT** ━━━━━━

There is no set rule about when to include the author's name in a text sentence and when to refer to it only in the parenthetical citation. Either way is acceptable. Write what seems most natural to you. Your goal is simply to identify clearly the source of the quotation or paraphrase.

*Part of a Work with Many Volumes*

- **Cite the volume number followed by a colon and the page number(s). Don't write the words *volume* or *page*.**

In <u>Contemporary Literary Criticism</u>, many critics, among them American poets Stanley Kunitz and W.D. Snodgrass, comment on and analyze Roethke's poetry (8: 455, 459).

To cite an entire volume in a parenthetical citation, write the author's name, a comma, and the abbreviation *vol.*

Kennedy's October 22 speech electrified the world; you can relive those moments on video-tape (20th Century History, vol. 4).

*Two or More Works in a Single Citation*

- **Separate the citations with a semicolon.**

Thirty years later, reporters interviewed and wrote about people who had played crucial roles in the crisis, among them U.S. General Curtis LeMay and journalist John Scali (Rhodes; Hernandez).

*Quotation from an Indirect Source*

- **If you are quoting from an indirect source, write the abbreviation *qtd. in* before the source. Whenever possible, however, try to quote from the original source. Sometimes, as in the following example, the original source is not available and you have to credit an indirect source.**

"Better to have met the issue squarely in Cuba," an editorial in the <u>Boston Herald</u> proclaimed, "than later in Berlin or Turkey or even Paris" (qtd. in "Excerpts").

*Literary Work*

- **For prose works that appear in many different editions, cite the chapter (ch.), part (pt.), or section (sec.) number.**

In Charles Dickens's <u>David Copperfield</u>, the villainous Uriah Heep threatens his employer, Mr. Wickfield, with what he knows: "Let sleeping dogs lie—who wants to rouse 'em? I don't. Can't you see I am as umble [humble] as I can be?" (ch. 39).

- **Cite the act and scene numbers of plays: *(Hamlet* II.i) or *(Hamlet* 2.1).**

On hearing that his wife is dead, Macbeth grapples with the meaning of life:

```
Life's but a walking shadow, a poor player
That struts and frets his hour upon the
     stage,
And then is heard no more; it is a tale
Told by an idiot, full of sound and fury,
Signifying nothing.  (Macbeth V.v)
```

■ **Cite the line numbers of poems: ("Intimations" 1-4).**

```
Roethke recalls his student Jane, who died
when she was thrown from a horse, "And how,
once startled into talk, the light syllables
leaped for her,/ And she balanced in the
delight of her thought" ("Elegy for Jane" 3-4).
```

**HINT**

If you need to insert a citation that is not covered by any of these style rules, refer to the *MLA Handbook for Writers of Research Papers*, 4th edition.

**EXERCISE 1** What's Wrong with These Citations?

Fix them. Pay careful attention to placement, content, and punctuation. Write the sentence, with the citation, on the lines provided. (Hint: You will not need all of the information given.)

**1.** Also, Alice and Siddhartha both went through an initiation, an increased awareness of the world. For Alice, it was when she realized that the Queen and her court were "nothing but a pack of cards," (this quote is in Chapter 12 of *Alice's Adventures in Wonderland*, which appears in many different editions), not authority figures to be respected and obeyed without question.

_____

_____

_____

**2.** For Siddhartha, the initiation came when he stopped believing that the world was illusory and superficial, when he saw that "Meaning and reality were not hidden somewhere behind things, they were in them, in all of them." (*Siddhartha* by Herman Hesse, translated by Hilda Rosner, published by New Directions in 1951, page 32)

_____

_____

_____

## EXERCISE 2 Be a Peer Editor

Give this writer a hand by correcting all mistakes in parenthetical citations. Follow the MLA style of parenthetical documentation. This is a good exercise to do with a partner or small group—if that is okay with your teacher. (Hint: when a poem's title is mentioned in the text, cite only line numbers.)

The poetry of Theodore Roethke (1908-1963) has other literary influences. Stanley Kunitz notes "throwbacks" to nursery rhymes, folk literature, counting songs, the Bible, and Blake. "But," he adds, "the poems, original and incomparable, belong to the poet and not his sources." (Stanley Kunitz, pages 102 and 103. A further influence is the poetry of both T.S. Eliot and W.B. Yeats. In Roethke's <u>Words for the Wind</u>, for instance, the poem "The Dying Man" is "in a voice almost indistinguishable from Yeats's" (W.D. Snodgrass, pp. 104-105). Some critics have attacked Roethke's imitation of Yeats, calling it a sign of weakness on Roethke's part and a lack of his own ideas and insight (Ralph J. Mills, Jr., page 30).

Roethke's poems are intensely personal. He takes the evolution of self as a theme in much of his poetry, occasionally relating it to another, or a beloved. (Pages 30 and 31 in Mills). An example of the self theme is found in the poem "Open House":

> My secrets cry aloud.
> I have no need for tongue.
> My heart keeps open house,
> My doors are widely swung.
> An epic of the eyes
> My love, with no disguise.

(These are lines 1-6 from the poem "Open House." I found this poem on page 718 in <u>The New Oxford Book of American Verse</u>, edited by Richard Ellmann, © 1976, Oxford University Press.)

## Writing Parenthetical Citations

In the space provided write a parenthetical citation for the work or works given. Read each numbered item carefully before you write the citation. Much more information is provided than you will need. You will have to figure out what information is relevant. Provide only the information required, and be sure to enclose the citation in parentheses.

**1.** A quotation from page 120 of an article entitled "Hoop Dreamer" about Mannie Jackson, owner of the Harlem Globetrotters. The article was written by Brad Herzog and appears in *Sky Magazine*, April 1996, pp. 119-123.

**2.** An article entitled "Eskimo" on page 891 of the Columbia Encyclopedia, 5th edition, 1993. No author is listed.

**3.** An editorial in the *Miami Herald* on May 22, 1996 on page 14, section A. The title of the editorial is "The Habit of Free Elections." No author is cited.

**4.** A paraphrase of an idea in an article by Neil Strauss. The article is titled "Rock Outdoors: An Endangered Species." It appeared in *The New York Times*, Sunday, May 12, 1996, Arts & Leisure, Section H, p. 44, southern edition.

**5.** *Women's Rights in the United States: A Documentary History*. The editors are Winston E. Langley and Vivian C. Fox. The citation refers to a chart near the beginning of the book, entitled "Significant Dates in the History of Women's Rights," which appears on pages xxxi-xxxiii.

**6.** A reference to the entire book *The Diversity of Life* by Edward O. Wilson. *The Diversity of Life* was published in 1992 by the Harvard University Press.

**7.** A quotation from *500 Nations: An Illustrated History of North American Indians* by Alvin M. Josephy, Jr., published in New York by Alfred A. Knopf in 1994. The reference is to material entitled "A Clash in the Arctic," pp.173-181. Josephy's name appears in the sentence that ends with the citation.

**8.** A quotation (lines 14-17) from a poem by Theodore Roethke entitled "Elegy for Jane." The research paper cites six other poems by Roethke.

**Writing Parenthetical Citations for Your Paper**

Change each of the temporary citations in your draft to their proper form. List each citation on the lines below. When you write your citations in your draft, check the placement, content, and punctuation of each citation.

_____

_____

_____

_____

_____

_____

_____

_____

_____

_____

## Works Cited List or Bibliography

**Prepare your Works Cited list, an alphabetical list of all the sources you have referred to in your paper. Place the Works Cited list at the end of your research paper.**

The entries in this chapter follow the MLA style for documenting sources, which is the style most often required by high school and college teachers. A different style of documentation, the APA style (see Appendix B), is used in psychology journal articles and is required for college psychology papers. Be sure to follow exactly the style of documentation your teacher requires.

Arrange entries on the Works Cited list alphabetically, and follow the style shown on pages 96–97.

The style for entries in the Works Cited list is exactly the same as the style you used for bibliography source cards in Step 2 (see pages 28–31). You do not have to memorize the style; you just have to know where to

find it so you can refer to it when you have a question about style.

To prepare your Works Cited list, all you have to do is to put your bibliography source card entries in alphabetical order and write them on a separate sheet of paper at the end of your research paper. The Works Cited list should contain entries for _every source you actually use_ in your paper—_not_ every source you consulted. Your source card list will probably be much longer than your final Works Cited list.

Instead of a Works Cited list, your teacher may require a **bibliography**, which lists _all of the sources you consulted_ while doing your research. A bibliography follows exactly the same format and style as a Works Cited list. Use the Works Cited list on the next page as a model for proper form when you compile your own Works Cited list or bibliography.

# Works Cited

"The Blockade: The U.S. Puts It on the Line." Life 2
Nov. 1962: 35.

Bonafede, Dom. "Refugees' Hopes Get a Big Boost." Miami
Herald 24 Oct. 1962, sec. A: 2.

Craig, Gordon A. and Alexander L. George. Force and
Statecraft New York: Oxford UP, 1990.

"Cuba and the Future." Life 9 Nov. 1962: 4.

"The Cuban Missile Crises, 1962, A Chronology of
Events." The National Security Archive.
George Washington U. 28 Dec. 1996 <http:///www.
seas.gwu.edu/nsarchive/nsa/cuba_mis_cri/cmcchron4>

Davis, Jerry C. Letter. Time 9 Nov. 1962: 7.

"Excerpts from Newspaper Editorials on Decision to
Impose Arms Blockade on Cuba." New York Times 24 Oct.
1962, sec. 1: 26. Originally appeared in Boston
Herald.

Finkelstein, Norman H. Thirteen Days/Ninety Miles: The
Cuban Missile Crisis. New York: Julian Messner, 1994.

Grunwald, Joseph. Personal interview. 2 Dec. 1995.

---. E-Mail to the author. 7 Jan. 1996.

Herblock. Cartoon. Newsweek 12 Nov. 1962: 25.
Originally appeared in Washington Post.

Kennedy, John F. "Text of Kennedy's Address on Moves to
Meet the Soviet Buildup." New York Times 23 Oct.
1962, sec.1: 18.

Kennedy, Robert F. Thirteen Days: A Memoir of the Cuban
Missile Crisis. New York: Norton, 1969.

"The Lessons Learned." Newsweek 12 Nov. 1962: 21.

"Munich Pact." The Columbia Encyclopedia. 5th ed. New
York: Columbia UP, 1993.

"A New Resolve to Save the Old Freedoms." Life 2 Nov.
1962: 4.

"Other Pressure Points." Life 9 Nov. 1962: 47.

Reston, James. "Khrushchev's Misjudgment on Cuba." New
York Times 24 Oct. 1962, sec. 1: 38.

Robbins, Dale. Letter. New York Times 25 Oct. 1962,
sec. 1: 38.

Robertson, Nan. "Anxiety Coupled with Support Here on
U.S. Move." 24 Oct. 1962, sec. 1: 26.

Schwartz, Barry W. Letter. <u>Miami Herald</u> 24 Oct: 1962, sec. A: 6.

"Showdown-Backdown." <u>Newsweek</u> 5 Nov. 1962: 28.

Sulzberger, C.L. "Foreign Affairs: U.S. Policy Trends: III-Showdown." <u>New York Times</u> 24 Oct. 1962, sec. 1: 38.

Thompson, Robert Smith. <u>The Missiles of October: The Declassified Story of John F. Kennedy and the Cuban Missile Crisis</u>. New York: Simon & Schuster, 1992.

Walker, William. Letter. <u>Newsweek</u> 12 Nov. 1962: 4.

"What Happened in the Kremlin?" <u>Newsweek</u> 12 Nov. 1962: 26.

**HINT**

What if you're missing information about one or more of your sources? Page numbers? Year of copyright? City of publisher? You'll have to go back to the library—or wherever you located your source—and find the missing information. If you were very careful preparing your bibliography source cards, you won't have to make the annoying last-minute trip.

**EXERCISE**

## What's Wrong with Each of the Following Works Cited Entries?

Fix each entry. Refer to the style for writing entries on pages 28–31.

**1.** Williams, Trevor. <u>The History of Invention</u>. © 1987. New York: Facts on File.

**2.** "Top Crop of Free Agents Ripe for Picking" by David DuPree. <u>USA Today</u>. July 9, 1996. Page 3C.

**3.** James Conaway, <u>The Smithsonian: 150 Years of Adventure, Discovery, and Wonder</u>, New York, Knopf, 1995

**4.** Daniel McGinn. "I Spy a '98 Corvette" in <u>Newsweek</u>, 15, July, 1996. Pages 40-41

**5.** <u>The World Wildlife Fund Book of Orchids</u> by Jack Kramer. © 1989, New York: Abbeville Press

**6.** E-mail sent from Vicki Futscher to the author. This e-mail was sent and received on December 14, 1999.

**EXERCISE 6** **Writing Your Works Cited List**

On a separate sheet of paper, write a draft of your Works Cited list. Include all of the sources you have actually mentioned in your first draft. Alphabetize the sources and list them in the proper form. Exchange papers with a partner and check each other's lists for proper style (content and punctuation).

---

## CHECKLIST REVIEW

☑ Follow the style of documentation your teacher specifies.

☑ Give credit for every quotation and paraphrase.

☑ Prepare your Works Cited list. Place the Works Cited list at the end of your research paper.

---

# Revise

*It is now time to revise your first draft. If you have kept to your schedule, you should have available to you sufficient time to do the job properly. It is important that you not rush through this critical phase of the writing process. Revising is the step that will transform a tentative, rambling first draft into a focused, coherent research paper. When you revise, you must look carefully and critically at what you have written, and it is nearly impossible to do that right after you have finished writing it. For this reason, it is a good idea to put your first draft away and not think about it for a while—at least overnight; an entire day or two would be even better. A little time away from your draft will give you "fresh" eyes and a more objective view when you sit down to revise.*

## Before You Start

Revising certainly does not mean just one quick rereading. You need several readings (a minimum of four or five), with time to think about problems you discover and time to come up with solutions. If you have followed the general guidelines in the timetable on page 137, you will have at least two full days of revising time. Use all of the time available to you. There is a lot left to do.

**Do It Yourself.** You need to do most of the hard work of revising—evaluating your paper's weaknesses and strengths and deciding what to drop, add, and change—yourself. The suggestions in this chapter offer a step-by-step approach to how to go about revising. Given enough time, you can vastly improve your paper.

# Computer Connection

Do your revising on a printed version (hard copy) of your first draft so you can "oversee" the whole paper instead of being able to look at just one screen at a time. Double or triple space to give yourself plenty of room to write in your changes.

When you have finished revising on your hard copy, you are ready to type your changes on the computer. Start by copying your first draft into a new document; call it version A or any other name you like. Then type in the changes you have made on the hard copy. That way, you won't lose anything in your earlier draft.

Also, remember to back up your revised versions onto disks—just in case your computer crashes.

**Peer Editors.** You can benefit from the feedback of peer editors at any point in the revising process. Usually, your first draft is so rough that it's not helpful to share it with anyone. Wait until you have revised your draft thoroughly at least once, and then exchange papers with one or more of your classmates. Read each other's papers carefully. Most of all, you want to know whether your readers understand what you are saying and whether they are confused or puzzled by any parts of your paper.

### Read your paper several times, focusing on a different aspect each time.

 Revising is a complex task with many parts, and it is impossible to look for everything at once. Force yourself to stay focused on one task at a time. Read through once for unity, a second time for coherence. Start from the beginning and focus on each paragraph, checking for topic sentences and adequate support.

Later, you will focus on each sentence and, still later, on word choices.

When you are revising, use the common proofreading symbols to indicate changes. Even though you are probably familiar with these symbols ( $\wedge$ indicates an insert; $\P$ means a new paragraph begins here), you will find them listed on the inside back cover of this book.

**HINT**

Looking for mistakes in grammar, punctuation, and spelling is the very last step in the writing process—proofreading (see Step 9). But if you spot a proofreading mistake as you're revising, fix it.

# The Paper as a Whole

**Check to see that you have met all of your teacher's requirements.**

Check the length of your paper, the number of sources, the parenthetical citations, the Works Cited list, and the manuscript form (see Step 10). If you haven't met all of the requirements specified in the assignment, you are asking for trouble. Talk with your teacher if you think your paper is running a page or two shorter or longer than the required length to see if it will still be acceptable.

# Computer Connection

If your teacher has specified a page length and your printed revised draft runs a page or so short or long, try adjusting your margins and line spacing a little to squeeze or stretch your paper into the required number of pages. This won't work for major cuts or stretches, however, which will require serious cutting or adding. If it is cutting you need to do, cut back wordiness rather than support. If it is adding you have to do, go back to your notes and see if you can find additional material that you haven't used.

**Focus on the paper's unity.**

The paper as a whole and individual paragraphs are said to have **unity** when everything works to develop the main idea of the paper.

**Does every main idea in the body of the paper relate directly to the paper's thesis statement?** Your outline should help you here because you dealt with this problem when you constructed the outline. Check what you have written against your final outline. If any paragraphs have wandered away from the "umbrella" of the thesis statement, either rewrite the paragraphs to bring them back under that umbrella or delete them entirely. Stay focused on your thesis statement.

**Does every sentence in a paragraph support its topic sentence?** When you are drafting, your thoughts may stray off course a little. It is time to delete anything that does not speak to a paragraph's main idea. (Check now, also, to see that each paragraph provides adequate support for the topic sentence.)

**Are you sure it is only one paragraph?** Sometimes a long paragraph seems strangely unfocused because it really should be broken into two separate paragraphs. Remember to begin a new paragraph whenever you start writing about a whole new idea, and make sure that each paragraph has a topic sentence. Note how the passage that follows has been revised to promote unity.

The American poet Theodore Roethke was greatly influenced by his childhood spent in the Michigan countryside, especially the time he passed in his family's greenhouse, observing nature. ~~Roethke, in case you haven't ever heard of him, was an American poet. He won many awards, and he died in 1963.~~ As a young boy Roethke spent a great deal of time working with his father and uncle in the greenhouse, and this seemed to impress itself on his mind. In later years, he tended to view himself and the world through green-colored glasses, seeing everything as related to and intertwined with nature. (Flowers, plants, earth, and greenhouse images appear in many of his poems.) One example of this greenhouse influence appears in the poem "The Minimal": "I study the lives on a leaf/ the little sleepers, numb nudgers in cold dimensions/ Beetles in caves, newts, stone-deaf fishes." ~~I really like the images in "The Minimal."~~ ¶ A second important influence in Roethke's life was the sudden death of his father in 1923 when Roethke was 15. His father's death seemed to tear apart Roethke's sense of peace and security. Roethke's deep hurt shows in much of his poetry. Critic Robert Boyers points out one example of the father's influence on Roethke's later work:

> In the poem "Otto," named for his father, Roethke recaptures the sense of pride he felt in a parent who controlled a rural environment immersed in the sounds and stinks and inconsistencies of nature. (209)

# EXERCISE 1

## What's Wrong with This Paragraph?

Revise the following passage, focusing on questions involving unity. Write your changes directly on the text. Hint: Consider breaking the passage into two or more paragraphs

Few people realize that the snake is not always a creature to be feared. Aside from sea snakes (all of which are water cobras and highly venomous), only about one-tenth of the world's snake species are poisonous. In the United States, according to the Merck Manual, the

fraction drops to about one-sixth (about 20
poisonous snakes out of 120 species). In the
United States more than 45,000 people are bitten by snakes each year, but fewer than 1 out
of 5 are poisonous bites, and only about 15
people die from snake bites each year (2565).
In fact, many snakes do a great deal of good.
"Snakes are of major importance as pest con-
trollers because of their extensive predation
on destructive mammals such as rats and mice"
(Columbia 2546). They also kill wild pigs,
small game in the jungle, and many harmful
insects. In many localities, especially in
India, the cobra, which is a highly poisonous
snake, is held sacred and therefore leads an
almost semidomesticated life. More than 20,000
deaths in India each year are attributed to the
bite of poisonous snakes. According to Hegner,
the fact that a pair of cobras has come to live
under the floor of the village temple is a good
omen rather than an evil one (125). In fact, if
a cobra decides to settle down in your house it
is considered a sign of prosperity. In Europe,
white storks are also considered good luck, and
people build platforms on their roofs so storks
will build their nests there (Columbia 2628). A
dish of water or milk is put near the cobras'
lair each day, and no one disturbs them, for
they help to kill the rats, which are a real
pest in most Indian villages. "Of course,"
Hegner reports, "accidents do happen, and some
people who step carelessly are bitten and die"
(126). My cousin Jerrod stepped on a black
snake once, but nothing happened to him.

## Revising for Unity

In one sitting, revise your first draft, focusing only on unity. You may want to read through your whole draft once and then carefully reread each paragraph.

## Coherence

A paper has **coherence** when the ideas are clearly and logically presented and the writer's thoughts are easy to follow.

> **Focus on the paper's coherence.**
> Check to see that ideas are presented in a logical order.

You have already thought about the order of ideas as you planned your outline, but sometimes the actual writing reveals an order that seems more logical. (Any order is logical if it makes sense to the reader.) If you are writing about a topic that has a history, you will probably present your information chronologically—moving from past to present and maybe on to the future. Or you might present your ideas in the order of importance, or moving from general to specific or in a problem-solution or cause-effect sequence.

If your revisions involve reordering paragraphs or sentences, try reading them aloud to see how the new order sounds. You can use the cut-and-paste commands on a computer to see how your rearranged paragraphs read.

**Use devices to help ensure coherence: parallel structure, repetition of key words, transitional expressions.** You know these devices from the writing you have been doing throughout your school career. They are important because they help readers follow your thinking.

```
PARALLEL STRUCTURE

The poems "Bright Star" by John Keats and

Robert Frost's "Choose Something Like a Star"
by Robert Frost
ʌboth discuss certain qualities in a star that
                                    a person.
may be desirable in ʌhuman beings.
                      ʌ

REPETITION OF KEY WORDS

Keats is much more flowery and tends to use
                        language
softer, more flowing words, as when he talks

about a "soft fall and swell" on the "new

soft-fallen waste of snow." Frost, however,
                          _  _        uses        r
is much ʌmore downʌtoʌearth and is more simpleʌ
          more language.    Frost's
and ʌdirectʌ When the star says, "I burn," the
     ʌ              ʌ
speaker's response is, "Talk Fahrenheit, talk
              Frost's
Centigrade." The speaker asks the star to
              ʌ
```

```
                                              Frost
"use language we can comprehend," and that is
exactly what the poet does.
```

**CLEAR PRONOUN REFERENCE**

```
Frost                   Keats's
The poet alludes to his star in his poem, but
Frost's
his vision of a star is distinctly his own,
                   the
and in the end both poets reach separate con-
clusions.
```

**TRANSITIONAL EXPRESSIONS**

```
On the other hand,
   Frost, instead of just choosing a quality in
a star that he likes, is waiting for some
                 At first
sort of message. The star will only say "I
         in the end, it
burn," but tells us that we should not only
              (like Keats's star)
be steadfast but have a certain loftiness

as well.
```

Here is a list of some useful transitional words and phrases grouped according to the logical relationships they suggest.

## Transitional expressions

**Showing importance:** above all, first (second, third, etc.), last, mainly, more important, most important, to begin with

**Showing time order:** after, at last, at the same time, before, during, eventually, finally, first (second, third, etc.), later, meanwhile, next, once, soon, then, when, whenever, while

**Showing cause and effect:** as a result, because, consequently, for, in effect, since, so, so that, thus, therefore

**Showing comparison:** also, and, another, besides, both, in like manner, like, moreover, not only—but also, similarly, still, too

**Showing contrast:** although, but, despite, however, in contrast, in spite of, nor, nevertheless, on the other hand, on the contrary, still, yet

**Showing an explanation:** for example, for instance, in fact, in other words, specifically, that is, thus, to illustrate

## EXERCISE 3   Revising for Coherence

Revise the following passage, writing your changes directly on the text. Compare your corrections with those of your classmates. Does everyone agree on what the problems are? Have you suggested different revisions?

> Everyone dreams, and only a small percentage of those dreams are remembered. There are many theories about what causes dreams. Some psychologists think that dreams are a window into the subconscious, an important sign of inner thoughts and buried feelings (4). Sigmund Freud believed that dreams represent wish-fulfillments. Some insist that dreams are a forgetting process, a way to get rid of unwanted or annoying emotions. An exciting new theory proposed by scientists Francis Crick (who helped discover the DNA molecule) and Graeme Mitchison is that dreams are an "unlearning process by which the brain rids itself of unwanted impulses and associations" (5). Complex networks of cells in the cerebral cortex form faulty connections. During waking hours these give rise to fantasies, obsessions, and hallucinations. When people are asleep, the cortex is cut off from its normal input and output. The lower brain sends random impulses. These cause dreams (6).

## EXERCISE 4   Revising for Coherence

Read your whole paper once through for coherence. Then focus on each paragraph, and see if you can make your ideas easier to follow and understand. Insert transitional words and phrases wherever you think they will help clarify ideas.

# Sentences

**Focus on each sentence and on the way that related sentences work together.**

**Vary sentence beginnings.** The normal order of English sentences is subject + verb + complement(s), if there are any. (Direct objects, indirect objects, predicate adjectives, and predicate nominatives are all called **complements** because they complete the meaning of a sentence.) This order is built into your thinking; it is probably the way you talk. But if every sentence in your paper begins with the subject followed by the verb, your writing quickly becomes monotonous. Here are some ways to vary sentence beginnings.

- Begin with a **single-word modifier** (an adjective or adverb):

      <u>Certainly</u>, Henry David Thoreau's experiment at Walden Pond would have to be called a success.

- Begin with a **transitional expression**:

      <u>Of course</u>, one of the reasons Thoreau went to Walden Pond was to experience its extraordinary beauty.

- Begin with a **phrase**:

      <u>At the pond</u>, Thoreau says, he learned that as life is simplified, "the laws of the universe will appear less complex,..." Stripping his life to the bare essentials, Thoreau looked inward and outward and found what he was sure was the truth. <u>To understand Thoreau's experiment</u>, we must first understand the transcendentalist philosophy of Ralph Waldo Emerson.

- Begin with a **subordinate clause**:

      <u>When he returned to nature</u>, Thoreau found life beautiful and full of possibilities.

## HINT

Try reading your whole paper aloud to yourself, to a partner, or to your writing group. Sometimes you can *hear* problems—awkward or monotonous sentences—that aren't obvious when you're reading silently.

**Vary sentence length and structure.** In an average paragraph, some sentences will be short (especially those with the ideas you want to emphasize); others will be long. You don't have to count words or tally types of sentence, but it is important to create variety within your paragraphs. Remember that sentences can be classified into four types, according to their structure. (In the following examples, main clauses are underlined once and subordinate clauses are underlined twice.)

- A **simple sentence** has one main clause and no subordinate clause:

    Volcanologists are searching for a safe way to predict eruptions.

- A **compound sentence** has two or more main clauses and no subordinate clause:

    One new device analyzes gases from the plume of smoke above the volcano's crater, and it can be used from a safe distance.

- A **complex sentence** has one main clause and at least one subordinate clause:

    The inventor is a scientist who survived a sudden, violent eruption of a volcano in the Colombian Andes.

- A **compound-complex** sentence has two or more main clauses and at least one subordinate clause:

    Dr. Stanley Williams, who was taking measurements in the crater at the time of the eruption, survived, but six of his fellow volcanologists died when the volcano erupted.

### Combine a series of short, choppy sentences.

CHOPPY: English police officers are called Bobbies. They are named after Sir Robert (Bobbie for short) Peel. Peel founded the London Metropolitan Police. Irish police officers are called Peelers. They are also named after Sir Robert Peel.

COMBINED: English police officers are called Bobbies and are named after Sir Robert Peel, who founded the London Metropolitan Police. Irish police officers, also named after Peel, are called Peelers.

**EXERCISE**

## Revising Sentences

Read and revise the passage below. Vary the sentence beginnings. Combine some sentences to vary sentence length and construction. Feel free to reword, rearrange, and generally improve this paragraph. You may want to cut whole sentences, delete words, and change words. Get together with three or four of your classmates to share your revisions and talk about your changes.

There have been some great contributors to psychology. One of these was B.F. Skinner. B.F. Skinner was an American psychologist. He lived from 1904-1990. Skinner was a behavioral psychologist. Skinner believed that psychologists should study human behavior. They should not focus on concepts that can not be observed. Behavior can be shaped or learned. Skinner believed this. Behavior can be shaped with positive reinforcement. Positive reinforcement includes praise and rewards. It can also be shaped with negative reinforcement. Punishment and yelling are examples of negative reinforcement (Green and Sanford 186-87).

**Avoid wordiness and unnecessary repetition.** Don't fall into the trap of expressing your ideas in a wordy, convoluted way. Say everything as clearly and as directly as you can.

Migrating birds face many ~~all kinds and sorts of~~ obstacles, ~~when they are migrating~~. For instance, ~~one of the obstacles is a~~ lighthouses ~~which may~~ confuse birds, ~~and they'll often run right into the lighthouse,~~ which are attracted by their ~~lighthouse's~~ light. When the Washington Monument was first built, ~~in Washington, D.C.,~~ ~~it caused the death of~~ hundreds of small ~~flying~~ birds died ~~who lost their lives~~ when they crashed right into it ~~the Washington Monument~~. Migrating birds have also ~~unfortunately ceased to live when they have~~ crashed into newly constructed bridges and ~~brand-new~~ buildings, ~~that didn't used to be there.~~

# EXERCISE 6  Revising Everything There Is to Revise

Use all of your knowledge about revising to improve the following paragraph. Work especially on the way the sentences hang together. Write your revisions directly on this paragraph. When you have finished, copy your revised paragraph on a separate sheet of paper. Compare your revised paragraph with those of your classmates.

The book <u>A Connecticut Yankee in King Arthur's Court</u>, by the writer Mark Twain, tells about the story of a man from Hartford, a city in Connecticut, which is why the book's title refers to "a Connecticut Yankee." The man is named Hank Morgan. Morgan is struck on the head by a crowbar. A man named Hercules hits him with a crowbar. The two are fighting. After this happens, Morgan wakes up to find himself in the sixth century. Morgan was the foreman of an arms factory that manufactured weapons in 19th century Hartford, Connecticut. Morgan sets out to bring the civilization of the 19th century into King Arthur's Court in the sixth century. Morgan comes into conflict with an old man whose name is Merlin. Merlin is the court magician in King Arthur's Court. He also comes into conflict with the ignorance and superstition of the ordinary people who live in sixth-century England. Mark Twain's novel <u>A Connecticut Yankee in King Arthur's Court</u> appears on its surface to be a light and humorous adventure story. It is more than that. Mark Twain has written in this novel a parody of medieval English chivalry. (A parody is a humorous imitation.) It is also a parody of medieval English romance. It is an attack on social unfairness and political injustice. It is also an attack on human ignorance. Mark Twain also attacks human superstition.

**EXERCISE 7**

## Revising Sentences in Your Draft

Read through your draft again, focusing this time on individual sentences and on the way sentences work together in a paragraph. Vary the sentence beginnings. Combine some sentences to vary sentence length and structure. Reword, rearrange, and generally improve the sentences in each paragraph. You may want to cut whole sentences or delete words and phrases.

## Diction: Choosing the Right Word

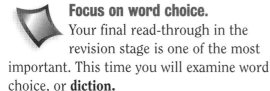

**Focus on word choice.** Your final read-through in the revision stage is one of the most important. This time you will examine word choice, or **diction.**

**Find the best word possible. Be precise.** The English language is very rich in synonyms, words that have almost the same meaning. Find and use the word that means exactly what you are trying to say. You can discover the different shades of meaning among synonyms and near-synonyms by checking a good dictionary.

**Watch your tone.** A research paper should be written in formal standard English—no contractions, no colloquial expressions, and certainly no slang.

**Avoid clichés.** Say it your way. Do not fall into the trap of using overworked, hackneyed expressions.

**EXERCISE 8**

## Focusing on Word Choice

As you revise this introduction to a research paper, focus on word choice. See if you can substitute precise words for vague terms. Revise the paragraph to give it a formal tone: replace or omit clichés, contractions, slang, and colloquial expressions.

```
    Imagine that you've handed over your
money to a big-shot accountant named Mr. Sam,
who's a guy with a good reputation. Mr. Sam
says he's going to take your money and invest
it so that when you stop punching the old
time clock, you'll have plenty of bucks to
support you through your golden sunset years.
However, one day when you least expect it,
you all of a sudden hear that Mr. Sam has
been using the money that was supposed to go
toward your pension for purposes of his own.
He's been paying off his bills, buying elec-
tronic stuff, and making loans to his bud-
dies. He says not to worry, he'll pay your
```

money back, with interest, when you need it.
Would you sleep at night with your money in
the hands of someone like Mr. Sam? Well,
folks, if you're currently holding down a
job, Uncle Sam is doing all of these things
with your money right this very second, as we
speak. Social Security funds are being used
to pay the government's bills, to build
weapons, and to make loans to foreign countries. To understand all of the hollering and
the yelling and fighting about the fate of
the Social Security Trust Fund and the future
of the entire program, it's a really great
idea to look up close at the background of
this extremely important and controversial
problem.

**EXERCISE**

## Revising for Word Choice

Read through your paper one last time, focusing this time on word choice.
Look for places where you can use more precise words. Eliminate contractions, colloquial expressions, slang, and anything else that detracts from a
formal tone.

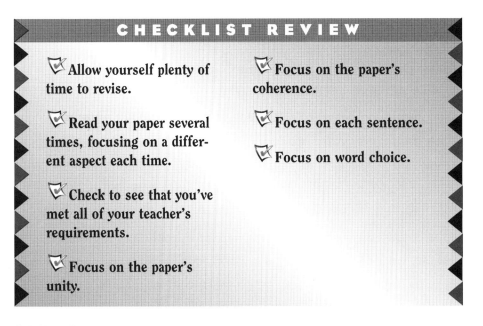

### CHECKLIST REVIEW

☑ Allow yourself plenty of time to revise.

☑ Read your paper several times, focusing on a differ-ent aspect each time.

☑ Check to see that you've met all of your teacher's requirements.

☑ Focus on the paper's unity.

☑ Focus on the paper's coherence.

☑ Focus on each sentence.

☑ Focus on word choice.

# Proofread

PEANUTS Reprinted by permission of USF, Inc.

**Y**ou are satisfied that the content and style of your paper are as good as you can make them. But your research paper is not quite done. Your final task is to sit down with your revised draft and proofread it for mistakes. When you proofread, you will focus on finding and correcting errors in spelling, punctuation, and grammar. Proofreading is much easier than revising, but it still requires your total attention.

## Before You Start

You will need ready access to a good college dictionary or an unabridged dictionary, and a grammar handbook or a handbook on usage. (See Appendix A, "What Every Good Research Paper Writer Needs.") You might ask your teacher if he or she has a preference about which dictionary and handbook you should use.

## Computer Connection

Learn to use the spelling and grammar checkers in your word processing program. Either look in the manual that comes with the program or use the Help menu within the program. These checkers can be especially useful since they may call to your attention errors in spelling and grammar that you have overlooked or of which you are unaware. Keep in mind, however, that these tools—though they are certainly helpful—cannot perform the proofreading task for you. A computer is not (and, some argue, will never be) a satisfactory substitute for a careful and painstaking reader.

# Proofreader's Symbols

 Learn to use the proofreader's symbols.

| SYMBOL | MEANING | EXAMPLE |
|---|---|---|
| ∧ | Insert | Cels are the basic units life. (of inserted) |
| ℰ | Delete (remove) | Plant cells have a a wall and chloro-plasts. |
| ℰ | Delete and close up | An egg is a single cell1. |
| ∾ | Transpose (switch) | Red cells blood carry oxgyen. |
| ≡ | Capitalize | all cells store genetic information in dna. |
| / | Make lowercase | We studied cells last year in Biology. |
| # | Add space | When I looked at a drop of pondwater through the microscope, I saw an amoeba. |
| ◯ | Close up space | The study of cell biolog y is called cytology. |
| ¶ | Start new paragraph | "Wow! Look at this!" Sue yelled, peering into the microscope. "Did you ever see anything so weird-looking?" Martin asked. |
| ⊙ | Period | Cells perform many important functions |
| ∧ (comma) | Comma | Plant cells contain chlorophyll but animal cells do not. |
| ∧ (semicolon) | Semicolon | Nerve cells transmit messages muscle cells contract to make movement pos-sible. |
| ◊ | Colon | Most cells have these three things a nucleus, a membrane, and cytoplasm. |
| = | Hyphen | An amoeba is a one celled organism that moves by changing its shape. |
| ∨ | Apostrophe | A plants green color comes from its chlorophyll. |
| ∨/∨ | Quotation marks | Your lab report is due tomorrow, Mrs. Merckel reminded the class. |

By the time you get to the proofreading stage, you probably will not have the time (or energy) to read through your paper several times. It is probably going to be once—or twice—through, focusing on everything there is to find during proofreading. So wait until you are awake and alert. (In other words, 3 A.M. the night before your paper is due is not a good time.) Proofread your revised draft; make corrections; and then type, write, or print a clean copy.

**Do It Yourself.** Give yourself enough time to sit down and read *word for word*—slowly. If you only look quickly through your paper, chances are your eyes will skip right over many mistakes. Slow your reading rate to a crawl, and concentrate. A quiet room and good lighting will help. If a word "looks funny" or sounds strange, consult a dictionary. Check punctuation, grammar, and usage questions in a grammar handbook.

Here are some proofreading techniques to try:

- Read your paper aloud to yourself. This will slow your reading and help you focus on one word at a time.
- Cover the text with a piece of paper and read only one line at a time. Focus on each word.
- Read the wrong way—from the bottom of a page to the top or from right to left.

**Another Pair of Eyes.** When you have found as many errors as you can, exchange papers with a classmate or two. A peer editor may spot mistakes you have missed.

## Spelling

**Check the spelling of words.** Students often complain, "How can I look up a word in a dictionary if I don't know how it's spelled?" Ask a friend or relative, or use your imagination and try several possible spellings. When you track down the correct spelling, be sure to add that word to your proofreading log (see page 117).

**Which word?** The English language has many homonyms, words that sound the same but are spelled differently and have different meanings. (For example: piece, peace; write, right; it's, its; wear, where; weather, whether) Make sure that you have used the right word in the right place. That is, make sure you have spelled a word correctly according to its meaning in the sentence.

## Computer Connection

A spelling checker stops at every word not in its dictionary (that includes most names and many other proper nouns) and sometimes makes silly suggestions. On the plus side, however, a spelling checker will catch *all* typographical errors in words contained in its dictionary, like *youself* when you meant to type *yourself*. A more serious problem occurs with homonyms. The spelling checker will not alert you to places where you have used *it's* for *its* or *accept* when you mean *except* or *already* when you mean *all ready*. Even if you use a spelling checker, you will still have to proofread your paper carefully.

**One word or two?** A compound word is made up of two or more words working together as a single unit (for example: high school, tabletop, ice cream, attorney general, cheerleader). Check a dictionary if you are in doubt about whether to spell such words as one word or two.

**Hyphenate or not?** Learn the rules for when to hyphenate compound words, and double-check in a dictionary if you are unsure. You will need to hyphenate compound numbers (thirty-one); some words beginning with the prefixes *ex-* and *self-* (ex-president, self-confidence); words ending with the suffix *-elect* (president-elect); and words in which a prefix comes before a capitalized word (all-American).

Double-check the spelling of all proper names (author's name, title, publisher, city) in your citations.

■ Make sure you have spelled the author's name exactly the way you spelled it on your bibliography source cards.

■ Make sure the author's name is spelled the same way in your parenthetical citations and on the Works Cited list.

**------- HINT -------**

Whether you are writing by hand or typing on a type-writer or computer, do not hyphenate words at the end of a line unless the word is spelled with a hyphen.

## EXERCISE 1  Proofreading for Spelling Errors

Cross out every word that is spelled incorrectly and write the word correctly in the space above.

REM sleep has been shone to have an important conection with dreams. REM, which stands for rapid eye movment, seems to be the sleep period when most or all dreams ocur. During a REM period, the subject's eyes move under closed eyelids, they're is a change in breatheing, and there are distinctive brain wave patterns. A REM period lasts any where from ten to ninty minutes and usually ocurs four to six times a night.

Experiments have been conducted in which patience were deprived of REM sleep. Researches watched the sleeping patience and wakened them as soon as rapid eye movments were visible. Subjects deprived of REM sleep were extremly iritable the next day and acted

as if they had recieved very little sleep,
even though they had all had their normal
amount of six to ten hours of sleep. After
five nites in a row of REM deprivation,
researchers aloud the subjects REM sleep. One
subject's first REM period, which would nor-
maly last about ten minutes, lasted sixty-
eight minutes. It was as if his body or mind
were making up for the lack of dream sleep on
the five previus nights.

## EXERCISE 2 — Checking the Spelling in Your Final Draft

If you have time to read your paper once through just for spelling, do it
now. Be especially careful to check the spelling of names used in your citations and Works Cited list.

## EXERCISE 3 — Creating a Personal Proofreading Log

On the lines below, record the words you misspelled in your first draft. If
you do not already have one, start your own personal proofreading log, a
list of errors you have found in your work. Besides spelling mistakes,
record other errors you have caught in proofreading—punctuation, capitalization, grammar, and usage. The next time you write an essay, review your
proofreading log *before* you begin drafting and also when you proofread.

_____    _____
_____    _____
_____    _____
_____    _____
_____    _____
_____    _____
_____    _____
_____    _____
_____    _____
_____    _____
_____    _____
_____    _____
_____    _____

# Capitalization

**Check your paper carefully to make sure you have observed the rules of capitalization.**

- **Start each sentence with a capital letter.**
- **Capitalize proper nouns and proper adjectives.** (For example: Willa Cather, U.S.S. *Missouri*; Cincinnati, Ohio; Norwegian salmon; Arabic numerals; French toast.)

If in doubt, check a grammar and usage handbook to review the rules for capitalizing and not capitalizing words.

## EXERCISE 4  Proofreading a Paragraph

Look for mistakes in spelling and capitalization as you proofread the following paragraph. Cross out incorrectly spelled words and write the correct spelling in the space above. Use the proofreader's symbol ($\equiv$) to indicate that a lowercase letter should be capitalized. Draw a slash ( / ) through a capital letter to make it lowercase.

> There are many ways to look at art, and in his poem "Museum piece," the american poet richard wilbur defines three attitudes. in the first stanza, the speaker describes the museum guards as "the good gray gauardians ofart"(1.3) They are ever-present, always hoverinbg about to make sure that nothing happens to any of the valueable Museum peices. They are "impartially protective," wilbur says(1.3) watching over every peace of Art with equal care, whether or not they agree with it's subject matter. Even tho they may be suspicius of the french artist Toulouse-Lautrec(1.4), they protect his paintings with as much attention as they give to anyone else's. The guards don't seem to care weather or not each peace of art is appealing to them. To them, Art is

an investment, to be watched over as carefuly
as one would watch over a fine car or even a
pile of money. Their is certainly respect in
this atitude, but no love and no feeling for
beauty. The whole tone of this first stanza
suggests a sort of dull reliability through
the use of the adjective "gray" and the
description of the spongy, comfortable shoes,
useful for the guards' endless pacing up and
down the museums hall ways.

## Punctuation

**Read through your paper and correct any errors in punctuation.**

- Indent each new paragraph. Here is a chance to give another look to each paragraph to make sure you haven't combined two paragraphs. Remember to cover each main idea in its own paragraph, complete with paragraph indent and topic sentence.

- Make sure each sentence has the appropriate end punctuation mark:

  Max Planck, a German physicist, developed the quantum theory, which suggests that light is neither waves nor particles but has properties of both ("Light" 191)⊙

- Place a parenthetical citation correctly in relation to punctuation marks:

In *The Universe in the Light of Modern Physics*, Planck asserts, "We have no right to assume that any physical laws exist, or if they have existed up to now, that they will continue to exist in a similar manner in the future." (393)⊙

- Use quotation marks correctly:

Albert Einstein, who developed Planck's theories further, stated in 1930, "The most beautiful thing we can experience is the mysterious. It is the source of all true art and science" (Einstein 39).

**EXERCISE 5**  **Proofreading Your Final Draft for Punctuation**

As you proofread your final draft, check every punctuation mark. Ask yourself these questions:

- Is each punctuation mark the correct one? (Be especially careful not to mix up colons and semicolons.)

- ■ Are there unnecessary commas? (Take them out.)
- ■ Has necessary punctuation been omitted? (Put it in.)

Add any punctuation errors—especially if you have made the mistake more than once—to your proofreading log.

## Grammar and Usage

**As you proofread your paper, correct any errors in grammar and usage.**

■ Check to make sure you have written complete sentences. Avoid sentence fragments and run-on sentences. A complete sentence has a subject and a verb, and expresses a complete thought. If any of these is missing, you have written a sentence fragment.

    **travels**
Light ~~traveling~~ at about 186,000 miles per second.

A run-on sentence has two or more complete sentences written as one sentence. A run-on sentence may have no punctuation or only a comma separating what should be two (or even more) sentences.

    Sound travels faster
    when air temperatures

are warm⊙ for example, at 20 degrees Centigrade, sound travels about 40 ft. per second faster than at 0° Centigrade.

■ Check to see that each verb agrees with its subject.

    Both the whale and the dolphin communicates by means of underwater sounds.

■ Check to see that the antecedent of every pronoun is absolutely clear.

    The lens and cornea are important parts at the front of the eye. **They**
    ~~It~~ focuses light on the retina at the back of the eye.

**EXERCISE 6**

## What Is Wrong with These Sentences?

Fix every mistake you find. Then rewrite each sentence correctly.

**1.** Henry David Thoreau, one of americas leading philosophers were a freind of Ralph Waldo Emerson, the essayist and poet.

_____

_____

_____

**2.** In 1845 Thoreau built a small wooden cabin on the shore of Walden pond and he lived their for almost too years.

_____

_____

_____

**3.** Of course one of the reasons he went to walden pond was to experience it's incredible beauty which he describes in <u>Walden</u> his book is based on the very detailed journal he kept while he lived in his cabin.

_____

_____

_____

_____

**4.** Thoreau had deeper motives tham merely appreication of natures beauty he believed as Emerson did that nature reflects the inner self and teaches us much about life.

_____

_____

_____

**5.** In Walden Thoreau tells of meeting a poor woodcutter who had very few material things but posessed a love of nature and was honest simple and content

_____

_____

_____

**6.** The essayist E B White called Walden "the only book I own". White said that he kept Thoreaus book handy "for relief" during times of despair.

_____

_____

_____

**7.** In the conclusion to Walden, Thoreau wrote, If a man does not keep pace with his companions, perhaps it is becuase he hears a different drummer Let him step to the music which he hears, however measured or far away.

_____

_____

_____

_____

**8.** Thoreau also wrote these wrods: "if one advances confidently in the direction of his dreams, and endevors to live the life which he has imagined, he will meet with a succes unexpected in common hours

_____

_____

_____

_____

**9.** Thoreau's essay "Civil disobedience," which he published in 1849 explained why he refused to pay the Massachusets poll tax.

_____

_____

_____

**10.** Both Mahatma Gandhi leader of India's struggle for independence from britain, and Dr. Martin luther king, jr. American civil rights leader was inspired by this essay

_____

_____

_____

_____

# Documentation

**Check your parenthetical citations against your Works Cited list.**

- Every work you have mentioned in a parenthetical citation should have a corresponding entry in the Works Cited list.

- Every entry on the Works Cited list should have at least one parenthetical citation in your paper.

- Double-check to make sure the entries in the Works Cited list are in alphabetical order.

**EXERCISE** **7** **Proofreading Your Final Draft**

If you have not proofread your entire paper, looking for all the kinds of errors mentioned in this chapter, do so now. Correct any mistakes you find, add them to your proofreading log, and type, write, or print your paper.

## EXERCISE  Proofreading—One Last Look

Don't turn in your final paper without another round of proofreading just to make sure that new errors have not crept in as you have made corrections. Read it one more time.

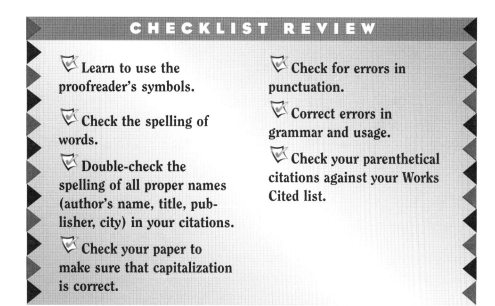

**CHECKLIST REVIEW**

☑ Learn to use the proofreader's symbols.

☑ Check the spelling of words.

☑ Double-check the spelling of all proper names (author's name, title, publisher, city) in your citations.

☑ Check your paper to make sure that capitalization is correct.

☑ Check for errors in punctuation.

☑ Correct errors in grammar and usage.

☑ Check your parenthetical citations against your Works Cited list.

# Prepare the Final Manuscript

Reprinted by permission: Tribune Media Services

Congratulations! You have kept plugging away at this monumental task, one step at a time. The hardest parts are behind you. Now you have only two things left to do: rewriting (or retyping or reprinting) your final paper and proofreading it one last time. If you have followed one of the suggested timetables on page 137, you should have plenty of time to finish before your due date. Don't try to finish your manuscript the night before your paper is due—something is sure to go wrong. Allow at least two days so that if disaster strikes on the first day, you will still be able to finish on time. Check to see that the equipment (typewriter, computer, printer) you plan to use is working and that you have on hand everything you can possibly need. Having a printer cartridge run out of ink or toner, or discovering that a typewriter ribbon is not black but red is a last-minute nightmare.

## The Paper's Form

 **Follow the format that your teacher requires.**

If your teacher has not specified any special requirements, follow these standard conventions:

**Paper.** Use 8 1/2" x 11" white paper. Do not use erasable paper because it smudges easily. Write or type on only one side of each piece of paper.

**Type, print, or write.** If you are using a typewriter, use a dark black ribbon. Test it first; you may need to buy a fresh ribbon and install it. A computer's printer should produce a dark copy that is easy to read. If you are writing by hand, use blue or black ink. (Make sure ahead of time that your teacher will accept a handwritten paper.)

# Computer Connection

Choose a typeface and size that are readable, and stick to them. You are not doing desktop publishing, so do not be tempted into banner heads and fancy typefaces. Keep the text plain, simple, and neat. Find out whether your teacher wants you to use italic type for book and magazine titles, or if you are expected to underscore all titles, as in the sample research paper on pages 126—136.

**Double-space.** Set your typewriter or word-processing program for double-space, and double-space the entire paper, including all quotations and the Works Cited page.

**Running head.** On every page, place a running head at the upper-right corner 1/2 inch from the top of the page and 1 inch from the right-hand edge of the paper. The running head consists of your last name followed by the page number. (See the model paper.)

**Heading.** The first page of your research paper has a four-line heading that lists your name, your teacher's name, the course title, and the paper's due date. Place the heading 1 inch from the top of the page. It is flush left (aligned with the left-hand margin) and above the title.

**Title.** Center the title above the text. If you have a subheading, be sure to use a colon. Do not underscore or italicize the title or enclose it in quotation marks.

**Margins.** Use 1-inch margins at the top, bottom, and sides of your paper.

**Indentation.** Each paragraph is indented 1/2 inch (5 spaces) from the left margin. In your Works Cited list, indent each turnover line 1/2 inch, too. Long quotations set off as blocks are indented 1 full inch (10 spaces).

**Hyphenation.** Do not hyphenate words at the end of a line.

**Page breaks.** Make sure you have at least two lines of a paragraph at the bottom of a page and also at the top of a page. This may require some juggling and/or short pages, but do not have single words or lines sitting by themselves. (These are called widows if at the top of a page, orphans if at the bottom.)

**Title page.** Usually, a title page is not required. If your teacher asks for a title page, however, follow his or her specifications for content and spacing.

**Get it all together.** Find out how your teacher wants you to put your paper together. A paper clip in the upper-left-hand corner is the easiest solution. Do not use a staple, pin, binder, or folder unless your teacher tells you to.

## Last But Not Least

**Proofread your final manuscript one last time.**

Be sure not to turn in your final paper (rewritten, retyped, or reprinted) until you have read through it one last time, just to make sure that new errors have not crept in.

**Make a copy.**

Before you turn in your paper, make a copy for yourself—just in case. You have worked so hard and so long that you should have a copy anyway.

## Sample Student Research Paper

The following paper uses the MLA style of documentation. A Works Cited list appears at the end of the paper.

Leslie Porter
Mr. Charles Fass
U.S. History
January 20, 1996

The Cuban Missile Crisis:
Immediate Responses and Lasting Effects

The Chinese character for the word "crisis" has two very different meanings. The first is the meaning we usually associate with the word in English: "a dangerous event or period." But the same character can also mean "opportunity." The fact that a crisis can actually have beneficial effects or can be the means for reaching a new understanding is often overlooked in international politics (Craig and George 129). The Soviets call it the Caribbean Crisis; the Cubans call it the October Crisis; to the rest of the world it is the Cuban Missile Crisis (Finkelstein 103-04). It is a crisis that brought the United States and the Soviet Union into their first direct confrontation of the nuclear age and drew the world to the very brink of nuclear destruction. By looking at the press coverage of the Cuban Missile Crisis at the time that it was happening, we can better understand the responses of Americans who lived through the crisis and how it changed their views. From our later perspective, we can also see that the crisis had important effects in both national and world politics.

A brief summary of the events from October 16 through October 28, 1962, is helpful in order to understand the importance of the crisis. On Tuesday morning, October 16, President John F. Kennedy received word that aerial photographs proved conclusively that the Soviets were building offensive--not defensive--nuclear weapons bases in

Running head 1/2" from top of paper

4-line heading: Name/Teacher/Class/Due Date

Title (centered); colon separates broad subject and limited focus

Introductory paragraph begins with attention-grabber about Chinese character for "crisis," opportunity.

Authors' names and page numbers for books on Works Cited list

General knowledge needs no parenthetical citation.

Thesis statement (here, two sentences) ends introductory paragraph

Background information (next three paragraphs)

Topic sentence

Events told in chronological order with many "time words" to clarify

Cuba. Kennedy and his advisors spent six days ———————— deliberating what the best course of action would be. They discarded the notion of an invasion of Cuba and settled on a blockade, which they decided to call a quarantine. According to Robert Smith Thompson, they chose the word "quarantine" because President Roosevelt had used it in 1937, urging "a 'quarantine' of Nazi Germany and Imperial Japan. Now, by using the word himself, JFK could wrap his Cuba policy in the mantle of FDR" (259).

News of the crisis first reached the American public on the evening of October 22, when Kennedy addressed the nation on radio and television. (It is eerie to look back at newspapers and magazines from October 16-21, when life seemed totally normal while the urgent probability of nuclear war was being discussed in the White House.) The President detailed the discovery of Cuban missile bases, announced the U.S. quarantine of Cuba, and promised that the U.S. would take further action if necessary. For the next several days, the world breathlessly awaited a direct confrontation that, luckily, never happened. Soviet Premier Nikita Khrushchev ordered Russian ships to turn around or avoid the American blockade. However, work on the missile bases continued. On October 26, Khrushchev sent Kennedy a letter offering to withdraw the missiles if the U.S. pledged not to invade Cuba ("The Cuban Missile"). The next day, a second letter arrived from Khrushchev, demanding U.S. withdrawal of missiles from Turkey. The U.S. ignored the second letter but responded affirmatively to the first, warning that withdrawal must take place by October 28 or the U.S. would conduct an air strike on Cuba. On October 28 Khrushchev announced the withdrawal of the missiles from Cuba. In his book <u>Thirteen Days</u>, Robert

General knowledge (now, not then)— needs no citation

Single quotes indicate quotation within a quotation.

Author's name cited in text; give only page number

Begin second paragraph of summary, which is too long for one paragraph

Writer's comment on her research experience, but no first-person pronouns used

Transitional word

Appositive identifies RFK

Kennedy, the President's brother and attorney general, revealed that the withdrawal had been verified with the help of the UN and aerial photographs (113).

Our actions regarding the Cuban crisis must be seen in their historical context. It is important to keep in mind that the crisis occurred soon after the Soviets built the Berlin Wall in 1961. We were still extremely concerned about the fate of West Berlin and were angry with the Soviets for their actions there. The Soviets were engaged in spreading Communism worldwide. Life magazine pointed out other "perilous points of confrontation": Turkey, Finland, India, South Korea, South Vietnam, Quemoy, Matsu, and Laos ("Other"). When Kennedy announced our Cuban blockade, U.S. officials were concerned that Soviets would retaliate in Berlin. They also feared that Red China, which supposedly had advisors in Cuba, would get involved in the crisis. JFK took the risk of confronting the Soviets, his brother wrote, because Cuba was just one arm of the Communist monster we were fighting all over the world (159). "Better to have met the issue squarely in Cuba," an editorial in the Boston Herald proclaimed, "than later in Berlin or Turkey or even Paris" (qtd. in "Excerpts").

One result of the Cuban Missile Crisis was a change in the way people and nations viewed President Kennedy. Joseph Grunwald, who lived in Miami at the time, remembers that before the crisis, people thought Kennedy was "immature, young, and inexperienced" and especially weak on foreign policy (Personal interview). During the April 1961 Bay of Pigs fiasco, hundreds of U.S.-trained Cuban exiles had invaded Cuba and been crushed by Castro's troops. Kennedy had refused air support to rescue them, and the CIA-sponsored invasion turned into a disaster. In fact, according to a <u>Newsweek</u> article, "until the test of will over Cuba, there had been large reservations about the President's capacity to cope with the unprecedented stringencies of the Cold War. The abortive invasion at the Bay of Pigs still haunted the nation" ("Lessons"). After the crisis, Kennedy's popularity and power increased greatly. He was seen as cool and level-headed under great stress, firm and decisive in protecting American interests and battling Communism. <u>Newsweek</u> summed it up: "Mr. Kennedy's behavior during the past two weeks has given Americans a sense of deep confidence in the temper of their President" ("Lessons"). Speaking for the four-year-old Cuban exile community in Miami, Humberto Medrano exclaimed, "We are with the President definitely, positively, and undoubtedly" ("Refugees' Hopes").

> Note that all of the magazine and newspaper articles cited were published during or immediately after the crisis.

> How the crisis changed views of Kennedy—positive views

> This paragraph provides four sources to support main idea.

Though Kennedy had the support of the vast majority of the American public, not everyone joined in praising him. Many Republicans pointed out that their party leaders had been warning of offensive weapons in Cuba for months. They claimed that JFK released the evidence when he did to influence the approaching Congressional elections. "I'll not vote for him," a New York salesman commented after the blockade was announced, "but I'll support him. His reaction was long overdue" (Robertson). A letter writer in <u>Time</u> pointed out, "If Mr. Kennedy had taken the advice of conservatives long ago instead of maligning them at every opportunity, the experience would have been much less traumatic for the American people" (Davis). Others charged that JFK's actions were too weak, that we should have pressed the advantage of being so close to home and invaded Cuba or tried to get rid of Castro. A <u>Life</u> editorial proclaimed, "For the safety

> Topic sentence: negative views of Kennedy

> Quotation interrupted for variety

> Note that this paragraph cites four sources to support main idea.

> Letters to the editor are listed on Works Cited page under writer's last name

and solidarity of this hemisphere, our objective must be to dismantle not only the missile bases but the regime" ("Cuba"). Similarly, a letter writer in The New York Times argued, "Sooner or later we are going to have to invade Cuba because it's the only way to settle the problem decisively" (Robbins).

    The crisis was almost uniformly seen as a tremendous victory for the United States in the Cold War. A November 2 editorial in Life proudly announced, "The Cuban blockade is a major turning point in the 17-year Cold War. The U.S. has dramatically seized the initiative" ("New"). We had taken a stand, made our position quite clear, and in the game of military chicken, the Russians jumped first. Not only was American public opinion overwhelmingly behind the President, but the U.S. got the support of its allies, including a 19-0 vote of confidence from the OAS (Reston). On the other hand, "the Soviet setback in Cuba clearly diminished Khrushchev's prestige in the Communist world," and Khrushchev was seen as discredited and handicapped ("What").

    The Cuban Missile Crisis made the ever-present fear of nuclear war dramatically apparent. This was nowhere more evident than in South Florida, only 90 miles from Cuba. The Miami airport closed, and the military arrived by planeloads and truckloads. Fearing nuclear attack, people descended on supermarkets for canned foods, water, candles, and batteries (Grunwald, E-mail). In a New York City on-the-street interview two days after Kennedy's speech, a Holocaust survivor commented that Americans "don't know what a danger they face in the Russians. Do they know that two hours from now or two days from now we could be involved in World War III?" (Robertson). "A full-scale blockade generally has been interpreted as an act of war," the

*Transition word*

*Topic sentence: second result/response—victory for U.S.*

*Transitional expression indicates contrast*

*Topic sentence: third result/response-fear of nuclear war*

*Interviewee recalls specific details.*

*Interviewee lived through World War II in Europe.*

<u>Miami Herald</u> reported ("Blockade"), and everyone feared what might happen. Finkelstein notes that there were secret government plans:

> At the White House plans were finalized for an evacuation of key governmental personnel and their families if Washington came under nuclear attack. Special passes were distributed and an assembly area was designated at the Reno Reservoir in northwest Washington, where a motorcade would be formed to transport people to the relocation area....The president himself did not consider leaving Washington (85).

A letter writer to the <u>Miami Herald</u> soberly warned: "John F. Kennedy will go down in history as one of this country's great Presidents--or its last--as a result of the [October 22] speech" (Schwartz).

The crisis showed the necessity of communication and direct negotiations between the superpowers. The whole concept of escalation suggested that events could very easily spiral out of the policymakers' control. In a letter to JFK, Khrushchev wrote that it would be dangerously simple for "matters to slide into the disaster of war" (Kennedy 126). Two weeks after the crisis had ended, a letter writer in <u>Newsweek</u> made this hopeful forecast: "The success of the Cuban blockade will truly prove a victory for all mankind if Russia and the U.S. will now sit down to serious and fruitful disarmament talks" (Walker). In fact, "the fate of man hinges on the willingness to communicate" ("Showdown" 28). Secretary of Defense Robert McNamara had to keep the military at bay:

> ...our quarantine was intended to be a political signal, not a textbook military operation, and trying to get that across to the military caused us all a lot of headaches. For twelve

days I lived in the Pentagon, from the 16th to the 27th, because I feared that they might not understand that this was a communications exercise, not a military operation (qtd. in Finkelstein 107).

One thing that emerged very strongly in contemporary response to the Cuban Missile Crisis was the immense concern with prestige and perception. Whichever side looked better in the eyes of the world had a better chance of keeping its allies and gaining new ones. Our decision to put up a blockade rather than invade Cuba was strongly influenced by the fact that we didn't think the invasion would have the support of our allies. "We have opted to force the issue ourselves," the Times' foreign policy columnist wrote, "without prior approval of our allies and there are going to be uneasy diplomatic moments" (Sulzberger). What really mattered was not who had how many missiles and where so much as the perception of who was stronger. Kennedy had made several speeches (including one on September 13 in which he stated that he would "do whatever must be done") warning that we would take action if offensive weapons were placed in Cuba. Not to follow up on these threats would have been to communicate to the Russians and to our allies that we were weak and would not honor our commitments. The American people felt, as the President did, that we were playing the role of right versus might and that the greatest danger of all was to do nothing (Kennedy 159).

The crisis reflected attitudes and lessons drawn from World War II. As Kennedy said in his October 22 speech, "The 1930s taught us a clear lesson. Aggressive conduct, if allowed to grow unchecked and unchallenged, ultimately leads to war." He was referring, among other things, to the Munich Pact of September 29, 1938, still a shameful memory almost twenty-five years later. In an

*Source where writer found quotation—not original source*

*Topic sentence*
*Fifth result—concern with prestige and perception*

*Topic sentence*

*More background information in this paragraph*

*Analysis of Kennedy's motivation*

attempt to avoid war, Britain and France had caved into Hitler's demands for annexing part of Czechoslovakia ("Munich"). The lesson that the Munich Pact taught was that it was important to be firm in the face of aggression. A cartoon reproduced in Newsweek, "The Other Road," made it clear that Kennedy would never say "peace at any price," but rather "war if necessary," even if the latter road was a much more difficult one (Herblock). In his October 22 address to the nation, President Kennedy had warned that we would react "to any other threat" or "any hostile move anywhere" against "peoples to whom we are committed."

The Cuban Missile Crisis had acted like a bucket of cold water thrown over the heads of world leaders, who were so frightened by the nuclear danger that they decided that negotiation and communication were of the utmost importance. As a result of the crisis, the following year the United States and the Soviet Union hammered out the Limited Nuclear Test Ban Treaty. Also, a special "hotline" was established for instant communication between the White House and the Kremlin. During the crisis, it had become clear that "seven-hour delays for messages to reach Washington and the reliance on bicycle-riding Western Union messengers were unacceptable means of communication in a nuclear age" (Finkelstein 109). These were perhaps the two biggest dividends of the Cuban Missile Crisis.

Observers at the time recognized that the Cuban Missile Crisis held tremendous significance for the nation and the world. "The ships of the U.S. Navy were steering a course that would be marked boldly on the charts of history," Life proclaimed, and "the steel perimeter clamped around Cuba by the U.S. could be the trip-wire for World War III" ("Blockade"). Newsweek predicted that the crisis "may turn out to have consequences of incalculable importance for this

Cites article in Columbia Encyclopedia

Cartoon idea supports paragraph; clear even though cartoon is not shown

Source of quoted material is clear [text of Oct. 22 speech] so parenthetical citation is not needed.

Transitional sentence

This paragraph deals with lasting effects of crisis.

First effect

Second effect

Details made known long after crisis

Topic sentence at end of paragraph

Topic sentence

Concluding paragraph —importance of crisis

century" ("Showdown"). Things could have turned out very differently than they did, but the prudence and caution of both Kennedy and Khrushchev altered this crisis into an opportunity for peace.

Writer's final observation refers to Chinese character for "crisis," "opportunity" in introduction.

Works Cited

"The Blockade: The U.S. Puts It on the Line." <u>Life</u> 2
     Nov. 1962: 35.

Bonafede, Dom. "Refugees' Hopes Get a Big Boost."
     <u>Miami Herald</u> 24 Oct. 1962, sec. A: 2.

Craig, Gordon A. and Alexander L. George.
     <u>Force and Statecraft</u>. New York: Oxford UP, 1990.

"Cuba and the Future." <u>Life</u>. 9 Nov. 1962: 4.

"The Cuban Missile Crisis, 1962, A Chronology of
     Events." <u>The National Security Archive</u>. 28 Dec.
     1996. <http:///www.seas.gwu.edu/nsarchive/nsa/cuba_
     mis_cri/cmcchron4>.

Davis, Jerry C. Letter. <u>Time</u> 9 Nov. 1962: 7.

"Excerpts from Newspaper Editorials on Decision to
     Impose Arms Blockade on Cuba." <u>New York Times</u> 24
     Oct. 1962, sec. 1: 26. Originally appeared in
     <u>Boston Herald</u>.

Finkelstein, Norman H. <u>Thirteen Days/Ninety Miles:</u>
     <u>The Cuban Missile Crisis</u>. New York: Julian
     Messner, 1994.

Grunwald, Joseph. Personal interview. 2 Dec. 1995.

——. E-mail to the author. 7 Jan. 1996.

Herblock. Cartoon. <u>Newsweek</u> 12 Nov. 1962:25.
     Originally appeared in <u>Washington Post</u>.

Kennedy, John F. "Text of Kennedy's Address on Moves
     to Meet the Soviet Buildup." <u>New York Times</u> 23
     Oct. 1962, sec. 1: 18.

Kennedy, Robert F. <u>Thirteen Days: A Memoir of the</u>
     <u>Cuban Missile Crisis</u>. New York: Norton, 1969.

Start new page.
Center title 1 inch
from top of paper.

Unsigned
article—alphabetized
by first word in title,
not including articles

Indent turnovers
1/2 inch.

Book title, two
authors.

Second author has
first name followed
by last name.

Online source: title of
document, Web site,
date accessed, and URL.

Unsigned magazine
article

Style for letter to
editor

Notes original source

Book title, one author

Personal interview
with writer

Indicates same author
or source as preceding
entry.

Style for cartoon

Colon separates title
and subtitle

"The Lessons Learned." <u>Newsweek</u> 12 Nov. 1962: 21.

"Munich Pact." <u>The Columbia Encyclopedia.</u> 5th ed. New York: Columbia UP, 1993.

"A New Resolve to Save the Old Freedoms." <u>Life</u>. 2 Nov. 1962: 4.

"Other Pressure Points." <u>Life</u> 9 Nov. 1962: 47.

Reston, James. "Khrushchev's Misjudgment on Cuba." <u>New York Times</u> 24 Oct. 1962, sec. 1: 38.

Robbins, Dale. Letter. <u>New York Times</u> Oct. 1962, sec. 1: 38.

Robertson, Nan. "Anxiety Coupled with Support Here on U.S. Move." <u>New York Times</u> 24 Oct. 1962, sec. 1: 26.

Schwartz, Barry W. Letter. <u>Miami Herald</u> 24 Oct: 1962, sec. A: 6.

"Showdown-Backdown." <u>Newsweek</u> 5 Nov. 1962: 28.

Sulzberger, C.L. U.S. Policy Trends: III-Showdown." <u>New York Times</u> 24 Oct. 1962, sec. 1: 38.

Thompson, Robert Smith. <u>The Missiles of October: The Declassified Story of John F. Kennedy and the Cuban Missile Crisis</u>. New York: Simon & Schuster, 1992.

Walker, William. Letter. <u>Newsweek</u> 12 Nov. 1962: 4.

"What Happened in the Kremlin?" <u>Newsweek</u> 12 Nov. 1962: 26.

Unsigned article in encyclopedia; page number not cited

Unsigned magazine article

Signed newspaper column; reporter's name followed by newspaper headline

Colon separates title and subtitle

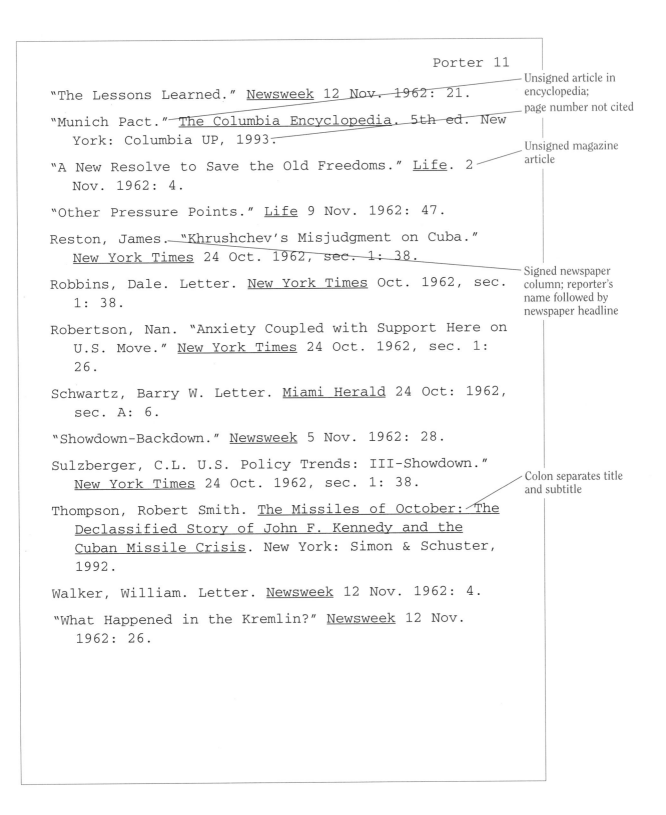

# Research Paper Paper Timetables

A research paper is a long-term assignment; in order to see it through to a successful conclusion, you will need to plan and keep to a schedule. Indeed, one of the most important aspects of a research-paper project is time management—making the most efficient use of the time available to you. Once you have been given the assignment and the deadline (the date on which you must turn in your finished work), your first order of business should be to draw up a project schedule. On the chart below you will find four timetables, each keyed to a different assignment span, that you might use as models to adopt or adapt, as best suits your own research paper.

START NOW

TURN IN YOUR PAPER

| Writing Process Stages | Prewriting | | | | | Drafting | | | Revising | Proofreading | |
|---|---|---|---|---|---|---|---|---|---|---|---|
| | STEP 1 Choosing and Limiting a Topic | STEP 2 Finding Sources | STEP 3 Taking Notes | STEP 4 Writing a Thesis Statement and Title | STEP 5 Writing a Final Outline | STEP 6 Writing the First Draft | STEP 7 Documenting Sources | STEP 8 Revising | STEP 9 Proof- reading | STEP 10 Preparing the Final Manuscript |
| **Time allotted by teacher varies. If total time available is** | | | | | | | | | | | |
| 10 weeks | 1 week | 3 days | 2 weeks | 3 days | 1 week | 1½ weeks | 2 days | 2 weeks | 2 days | 3 days |
| 8 weeks | 3 days | 3 days | 1½ weeks | 2 days | 1 week | 1 week | 2 days | 1½ weeks | 2 days | 3 days |
| 6 weeks | 2 days | 2 days | 1 week | 1 day | 2 days | 1 week | 1 day | 1½ weeks | 2 days | 3 days |
| 4 weeks | 1 day | 1 day | 1 week | 1 day | 2 days | 4 days | 1 day | 3 days | 1 day | 2 days |

137

# Appendix A

## What Every Research–Paper Writer Needs

When you write a research paper, you need three things that you cannot buy in a store or borrow from a library: curiosity, self-discipline, and perseverance.

In fact, the research paper assignment is designed to help you acquire these qualities if you do not already have them. As you work through Steps 1 through 10, pacing yourself to finish on time, you will be practicing the arts of self-discipline and perseverance.

You will need some tangible things, too, and these are easier to acquire. You will need access to an up-to-date encyclopedia, a college or unabridged dictionary, an easy-to-use thesaurus, and a grammar and usage handbook. You will probably find all of these in your school or local library or in your English classroom. However, it is a good idea to have a good college dictionary, a thesaurus, and a language handbook at home, too. They will come in handy for the rest of your life.

### A COLLEGE DICTIONARY

Many people talk about looking something up in "the dictionary"—as if there were only one. But there are hundreds of dictionaries of the English language in print. Some are extremely good; others are not. A good college dictionary will help you find or check all of the following:

- spelling
- capitalization
- plural forms
- irregular verb forms
- comparative forms for modifiers
- word origins (etymologies)
- idioms (expressions different in meaning from the literal meaning of the words)
- level of usage (for example: colloquial, slang, archaic, poetic)
- usage notes
- synonyms and antonyms
- biographical entries (spelling, pronunciation, identification, birth and death dates)
- geographical entries (spelling, origin of name, location, population, sometimes a little history)

Listed below are three of the best hardbound college dictionaries available. Resist the temptation to buy or use a paperback dictionary. Paperback dictionaries have fewer entries and scanty definitions, and they tend to fall apart after minimal use. If you are buying a dictionary, be sure to buy a hardbound *college* dictionary, not a *school* dictionary for young students.

- Agnes, Michael. Ed. *Webster's New World College Dictionary*. 4th edition. New York: Macmillan, 1999.

This college dictionary has been widely praised since it first appeared in 1951. It is the dictionary used by the Associated Press and by newspaper reporters all over the country as the standard for spelling and punctuation. Unlike other college dictionaries, this one was not based on an existing unabridged or earlier dictionary. The dictionary staff started from scratch, writing definitions, examples, and an easy-to-use pronunciation key.

- *Merriam-Webster's Collegiate Dictionary*, 10th edition. Springfield, MA: Merriam-Webster, 1998.

This dictionary includes a 24-page style handbook and is based on the authoritative *Webster's Third New International Dictionary*.

- *The American Heritage Dictionary of the English Language*, 3rd edition. Boston: Houghton Mifflin, 1992.

This large-format dictionary has more than 350,000 entries and more than 4,000 illustrations and drawings. Usage notes and regional American English notes provide up-to-date information about how words are used today in speech and writing. Houghton Mifflin also publishes *The American Heritage Dictionary*, *Third College Edition*, a standard-sized dictionary with more than 200,000 entries and many usage notes.

## A THESAURUS

The word thesaurus (thi ′sòr əs), from the Greek *thesauros*, literally means "a treasure." The lifetime hobby of Peter Mark Roget (ro ′zhā), an English doctor (1779-1869), was grouping words into categories. For fifty years, he organized all of the English words he knew and could discover into more than a thousand different categories of words related in meaning. He published the first thesaurus—his *Thesaurus of English Words and Phrases*—in 1852.

In book form, a thesaurus is a dictionary of synonyms and antonyms. A thesaurus is useful when you are trying to think of different ways to express an idea, when you want to avoid repeating the same word over and over again, and when you are searching for the word that best fits a context or shade of meaning.

There are almost as many thesauri available as there are dictionaries. Some require you to use an index, which lists several different categories (depending on the sense of the word you are using) where you may find synonyms in the book. These index-based thesauri are more difficult to use than a dictionary-type thesaurus, which simply lists an entry word and offers a variety of synonyms and antonyms.

There is no need to spend a lot of money on a hardbound thesaurus. Here are three good paperback versions that will serve you well.

- *Random House Roget's Thesaurus*. 2nd edition. New York: Ballantine Books, 1996.

In this easy-to-use paperback thesaurus, more than 11,000 main entries are alphabetized—just as they would be in a dictionary—with more than 200,000 suggested synonyms and antonyms.

- Morehead, Philip D. *The New American Roget's College Thesaurus in Dictionary Form*. Revised edition. New York: Signet, 1993.

This paperback combines the dictionary-style alphabetical listing and occasional larger-type entries for categories (as in the original Roget's Thesaurus).

- Laird, Charlton and Michael Agnes. *Webster's New World Thesaurus*. New York: Pocket Star Books, 1995.

Here is another easy-to-use, dictionary style thesaurus. This one was written by a contemporary American language expert.

If you are using a computer, you may have available one of the many word-processing programs equipped with a thesaurus. When you highlight a word in the text, the thesaurus suggests one or more replacements. (Suggested substitutes for *reliable*, for instance, might include *faithful*, *dependable*, *unfailing*, and *trusty*.) But a computer thesaurus is much less reliable than a thesaurus in book form. Sometimes it fails completely, as if it does not understand what you are asking it to do.

### A LANGUAGE HANDBOOK

When you write, revise, and proofread your research paper, you will find a well-organized language handbook extremely useful. Unless you are confident that you know all the rules for grammar, usage, punctuation, and capitalization (and who does?), it is a good idea to have a reliable "expert" to check with. Any of the hardbound handbooks listed here will last you a lifetime:

- Fowler, H. Ramsey et al. *The Little, Brown Handbook*. 7th edition. New York: HarperCollins College Publishers, 1998.

This thorough, easy-to-use handbook starts out with a section on the writing process and paragraphs. It devotes sections to grammatical sentences, clear sentences, effective sentences, punctuation, mechanics, effective words, the research paper, and special writing tasks (essay exams, business writing). There are features for ESL (English as a second language) students throughout the handbook. At the back there is a 20-page glossary of usage, an appendix on preparing manuscript, and another on writing with the word processor.

- Kirszner, Laurie and Stephen Mandell. *The Holt Handbook*. 5th edition. Orlando: Harcourt Brace, 1998.

This handbook is organized into nine parts, beginning with one on the writing process and paragraph skills. Succeeding sections deal with thinking critically, composing sentences, common sentence problems, using words effectively, grammar (with 20 pages on language issues for international [ESL] students), punctuation and mechanics, writing with sources, and writing in various disciplines.

- Hodges, John C. et al. *Harbrace College Handbook*. 13th edition. Fort Worth: Harcourt College Publishers, 1998.

This small, no-nonsense handbook has been around since 1941 (and revised regularly). It is hardbound, not quite pocket-sized, well designed, and easy to use. It has six sections: grammar, mechanics, punctuation, spelling and diction, effective sentences, and larger elements (which includes logical thinking, the paragraph, compositions, the research paper, and writing for special purposes). There is an 11-page glossary of usage at the back of the book. The research-paper section takes up a hundred pages, with two well-annotated sample research papers—one in MLA style, one in APA style.

## A BOOK ON STYLE

You can find dozens of books that attempt to teach the niceties of writing clear, graceful English. There is just one you should definitely read and—if possible—own:

- Strunk, William, Jr. and E.B. White. *The Elements of Style*. 4th edition. Boston: Allyn & Bacon, 1999.

This slim book (only 128 pages) first appeared in 1918. *The New York Times* calls it "as timeless as a book can be in our age of volubility." The authors give rules, examples, and sage advice on points they consider essential to good writing. The book's five sections deal with elementary rules of usage, elementary principles of composition, a few matters of form, words and expressions commonly misused, and an approach to style. The style section offers 21 sensible rules, such as "Avoid fancy words" and "Place yourself in the background." You can find the full text of William Strunk's original edition of *Elements of Style* (1918) online at <http://www.columbia.edu/acis/bartleby/strunk/>.

# Appendix B

## APA Style; Footnotes and Endnotes

Throughout this book, we have used the MLA (Modern Language Association) style of documenting sources because it is the style that most English teachers prefer. It is, however, not the *only* style. If you are writing a research paper for a social studies or science class, your teacher may ask you to use the APA (American Psychological Association) style. Or you may be asked to document your sources with footnotes or endnotes. On the following pages, you will find rules and examples for each of these methods of documentation.

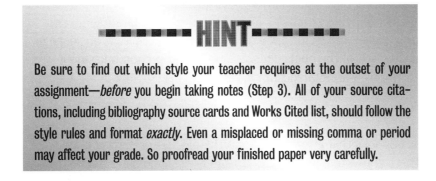

**━━━━━━ HINT ━━━━━━**

Be sure to find out which style your teacher requires at the outset of your assignment—*before* you begin taking notes (Step 3). All of your source citations, including bibliography source cards and Works Cited list, should follow the style rules and format *exactly*. Even a misplaced or missing comma or period may affect your grade. So proofread your finished paper very carefully.

## APA Style

The APA style is described in great detail in the *Publication Manual of the American Psychological Association* (1995). It is the style required for writers of college-level psychology and other social science papers and journal articles. It is also a style frequently used to report any type of original research.

An APA-style paper has several parts that an MLA paper does not have:

**1.** It always has a title page. Centered on the title page are the paper's title, the writer's name, the course name, the instructor's name, and the date the paper is being submitted. A key phrase from the title appears as the running head on the upper right-hand corner of every page. The same phrase is centered toward the bottom of the title page. Pages are numbered, starting with 1 for the title page.

**2.** Papers written in APA format always have an **abstract**, a concise summary of the main ideas covered in the paper. The abstract appears on its own page, after the title page and before the text of the paper. Often the abstract is one long paragraph; its first sentence is *not* indented. The word *Abstract* is centered at the top margin (one inch from the top of the page).

## Abstract

The Cuban Missile Crisis of October 16-28, 1962, threatened nuclear war but ended as an opportunity for peace. On October 16, President Kennedy received word that Soviets were building offensive missile bases in Cuba. Kennedy and his advisors spent six days deliberating what action to take. The public was not informed of the crisis until the evening of October 22, when Kennedy addressed the nation and announced a U.S. quarantine (blockade) of Cuba. After several tense days, during which nuclear war seemed a real possibility, Soviet Premier Nikita Khrushchev withdrew the missiles from Cuba. One result of the missile crisis was that Kennedy's popularity and power grew, although some conservatives criticized him for not taking stronger or earlier action against the Soviets in Cuba. The crisis was seen as a tremendous victory for the United States in the Cold War. It also spotlighted the fear of the real possibility of nuclear war. Another result of the crisis was the realization that direct communication and negotiation between the United States and the Soviet Union were essential to world peace. American responses to the crisis reflected our concern with how our Allies perceived us. In deciding to take a tough stance, Kennedy and his advisors drew on lessons learned from World War II. Two positive and lasting results of the Cuban Missile Crisis are the Limited Nuclear Test Ban Treaty of 1963 and the "hotline" established between the White House and the Kremlin.

**3.** The text of the paper begins on the page following the Abstract page. The text is double-spaced and each paragraph is indented. The paper's full title is centered at the top of the page. An introductory paragraph, which is not labeled with a heading, briefly introduces the topic of the paper and any findings or conclusions. Other sections of the paper may have headings, such as "Methods" (or "Methodology"), "Results," "Data," "Procedure," "Discussion," "Conclusions."

**4.** Following the text is a **References** page or **Reference List** (called a Works Cited list in MLA-style papers). It is an alphabetical list of all works cited in the text of the paper. Here are the APA rules for listing sources on the References page.

- Center the heading ("References" or "Reference List") two inches from the top of the page. Skip four spaces before the first entry.

- Double-space all entries. Use a hanging indent; that is, start the first line at the left margin, and indent three spaces all turnover lines for the same entry. (See the examples on pages 145–46.)

- Alphabetize all entries by author's last name. If the author is unknown, alphabetize by the first important word in the title (not the articles *the, a*, and *an*). Write the author's last name, followed by a comma and the initial or initials of his or her first and middle names. End the author information with a period.

- For two authors, list each, giving the last name first. Use the ampersand sign (&) between the authors' names. For more than two authors, use "&" before the last author's name.

- Following the author's name, write the date of publication in parentheses. Place a period *outside* the last parenthesis.

- Do not use quotation marks for the titles of articles, poems, or essays. Use regular type; do not italicize or underscore.

- Underscore titles of books, magazines, journals, and newspapers.

- For titles of all works cited, capitalize *only* the first word of the title and the subtitle and all proper nouns and proper adjectives. Keep all other words in the title lowercase and end with a period.

- When citing publishers, use an abbreviated form for the publisher's name (for example, Doubleday, *not* Doubleday & Co.), but give the full name of university presses (for example, Columbia University. Press, *not* Columbia UP).

If you record all of the information you need in *exactly the right style* when you are writing your bibliography source cards, it will be easy to do your References page at the end of your paper. In APA style authors' first names are not listed—only their initials. The citations also differ from MLA style in punctuation, capitalization, and placement of information. In the chart on page 145, you will find a summary of how APA and MLA styles differ.

| PART OF PAPER | APA STYLE/EXAMPLE | MLA STYLE/EXAMPLE |
|---|---|---|
| **TITLE PAGE** | Always has | Optional |
| **ABSTRACT** | Always has | Never has |
| **HEADINGS** | Usually has | Never has |
| **RUNNING HEAD AND PAGE NUMBERS** | Key phrase from title; page number on line below running head (flush right at top of page):<br><br>Cuban Missile Crisis 1 | Writer's last name followed by page number on same line (flush right at top of page):<br><br>Porter 1 |
| **SOURCES LISTED AT END OF PAPER** | References page. Indent turnover lines three spaces. | Works Cited list. Indent turnover lines five spaces. |
| **Book by single author** | Finkelstein, N.H. (1994). <u>Thirteen days/ninety miles: the Cuban missile crisis</u>. New York: Julian Messner. | Finkelstein, Norman H. <u>Thirteen Days/Ninety Miles: The Cuban Missile Crisis</u>. New York: Julian Messner, 1994. |
| **Book by two authors** | Craig, G.A. & George, A.L. (1990). <u>Force and statecraft</u>. New York: Oxford Univ. Press. | Craig, Gordon A., and Alexander L. George. <u>Force and Statecraft</u>. New York: Oxford UP, 1990. |
| **Book with single editor** | Chang, L. (Ed.), (1992). <u>The Cuban missile crisis, 1962</u>. National Security Archives: New Press. | Chang, Laurence, ed. <u>The Cuban Missile Crisis</u>, 1962. National Security Archives: New Press, 1992. |

## Parenthetical Citations

The APA author-date system of parenthetical documentation gives the author's last name, followed by a comma and the date of publication. When a specific page is referred to, a page number is also given.

EXAMPLES

A letter writer to the <u>Miami Herald</u> (Schwartz, 1962) soberly warned: "John F. Kennedy will go down in history as one of this country's great Presidents--or its last--as a result of the [October 22] speech." In fact, "the fate of

man hinges on the willingness to communicate"
("Showdown," 1962).

The Soviets call it the Caribbean Crisis; the
Cubans call it the October Crisis; to the rest
of the world it is the Cuban Missile Crisis
(Finkelstein, 1994, pp. 103-104). A November 2
editorial in <u>Life</u> (1962, p. 4) proclaimed,
"For the safety and solidarity of this hemisphere, our objective must be to dismantle not
only the missile bases but the regime."

Here are the rules for parenthetical citation in the APA style.

- Enclose in parentheses the author's last name, a comma, and the date of publication.
- When there are two authors, cite both authors' last names and connect them with the ampersand (&) sign. When there are more than two authors, give each one's last name, followed by a comma. Use the & sign before the last author's name.
- Cite the page number or numbers when a specific part of the work is referred to. Use the abbreviations *p.* (for page) or *pp.* (for pages) before the page numbers.
- When an author's name appears within the sentence of the text, do not repeat the author's name in the parenthetical citation.
- When the author is unknown, the parenthetical citation should give the first important word or words in the title of the work enclosed in quotation marks.

| PARENTHETICAL CITATIONS | APA STYLE | MLA STYLE |
|---|---|---|
| Book by single author | (Kennedy, 1969, p. 113) | (Kennedy 113) |
| Book by two authors | (Craig & Alexander, 1990, p. 129) | (Craig and Alexander 129) |
| Book by three or more authors | (Bullock, Stallybrass, & Trombley, 1995) | (Bullock, Stallybrass, and Trombley) |
| Book by single editor | (Chang, 1990, p. 154) | (Chang 154) |
| Magazine or newspaper article (signed) | (Robertson 1962) | (Robertson) |
| Magazine or newspaper article (unsigned) | ("Blockade," 1962) | ("Blockade") |
| Encyclopedia article (unsigned) | ("Munich," 1993, p. 1857) | ("Munich" 1857) |

# Footnotes and Endnotes

Before the 1980s (when parenthetical citations were first introduced), all research paper writers used either footnotes or endnotes to document their sources. With these systems, quotations or paraphrases that need documentation are indicated by a superscript (raised) number following the quotation or paraphrase. This number refers the reader to the place where full information about the source is given. When the full documentation appears at the bottom of the page, it is called a **footnote**. When it appears on a separate sheet at the end of the paper, it is called an **endnote**.

Both footnotes and endnotes may also be used for additional comments or explanations that would interrupt the sense of the text. Used for this purpose, they are called **content notes**.

Footnotes and endnotes follow exactly the same style. The content and order of information is similar, but not identical, to the MLA style for entries on the Works Cited list. Here, for example, is one paragraph of the Cuban Missile Crisis paper along with the footnotes at the bottom of the page. Notice that in the text the superscript number appears immediately following the punctuation mark.

EXAMPLE

> The crisis was almost uniformly seen as a tremendous victory for the United States in the Cold War. A November 2 editorial in <u>Life</u> proudly announced, "The Cuban blockade is a major turning point in the 17-year Cold War. The U.S. has dramatically seized the initiative."[6] We had taken a stand, made our position quite clear, and in the game of military chicken, the Russians jumped first. Not only was American public opinion overwhelmingly behind the President, but the U.S. got the support of its allies, including a 19-0 vote of confidence from the OAS.[7] On the other hand, "the Soviet setback in Cuba clearly diminished Khrushchev's prestige in the Communist world," and Khrushchev was seen as discredited and handicapped.[8]
>
> ---
>
> [6]"A New Resolve to Save the Old Freedoms," <u>Life</u> 2 Nov. 1962: 4.
>
> [7]James Reston, "Khrushchev's Misjudgment on Cuba," <u>New York Times</u> 24 Oct. 1962, natl: ed., sec. 1: 38.
>
> [8]"What Happened in the Kremlin?" <u>Newsweek</u> 12 Nov. 1962: 26.

## Guidelines for Placement of Footnotes and Endnotes

### Both Footnotes and Endnotes

- Number the footnotes or endnotes consecutively throughout the paper.
- Place a superscript (raised) Arabic number immediately *after* a quotation or paraphrase, leaving no space between a word or punctuation mark and the number.

### Footnotes Only

- Separate the footnote(s) from the text of the paper with four lines of space or with a 12-space rule from the left margin (as in the example on page 147).
- Indent each footnote five spaces. Start turnover lines at the left margin. Begin with the superscript number, *followed by one space*, and give the information in the order shown on the chart below. Be sure to follow the punctuation exactly.
- Single-space the text of each footnote. If more than one footnote appears on a page, use two lines of space (a double space) between footnotes.

### Endnotes only

- Place the superscript numbers for endnotes in the text exactly as they are for footnotes.
- Document all endnotes, numbered consecutively, on a separate page or pages at the end of the paper.
- Center the word *Notes* one inch from the top of the page. Use three lines of space between this heading and the first note. Unlike footnotes, endnote entries are double-spaced.
- Indent each note five spaces. Turnover lines are flush left with the margin. Begin with the superscript number, *followed by one space*, and give the information in the order shown in the chart on the facing page. Be sure to follow the punctuation exactly.

| STYLE FOR FOOTNOTES OR ENDNOTES | |
|---|---|
| **Book by single author** | [1] Norman H. Finkelstein, <u>Thirteen Days/Ninety Miles: The Cuban Missile Crisis</u> (New York: Julian Messner, 1994). |
| **Book by two authors** | [2] Gordon A. Craig and Alexander L. George, <u>Force and Statecraft</u> (New York: Oxford Univ. Press, 1990) 132. |
| **Book with single editor** | [3] Laurence Chang, ed., <u>The Cuban Missile Crisis, 1962</u> (National Security Archives: New Press, 1992). |
| **Newspaper or magazine article (unsigned)** | [4] "The Lessons Learned," <u>Newsweek</u> 12 Nov. 1962: 21. |
| **Newspaper or magazine article (signed)** | [5] James Reston, "Khrushchev's Misjudgment on Cuba," <u>New York Times</u> 24 Oct. 1962: A38, cols. 3–4. |
| **Encyclopedia article (unsigned)** | [6] "Munich Pact," <u>Columbia Encyclopedia</u>, 1993 ed. |

# Appendix C

## Writing Across the Curriculum

You may find a research paper assigned in your social studies or science class, and sometimes in other classes, too. The movement to add substantial writing assignments in classes other than English is a result of a widespread effort to improve students' writing and thinking skills. The "writing across the curriculum" movement began in the 1970s and quickly became established at all levels of schooling—from elementary through college. Teachers in subjects other than English generally give no instruction in how to go about writing research papers. They assume that you already know all you need to know from your English classes.

Usually, an assignment by a social studies or science teacher is quite specific. Here are some examples:

### SOCIAL STUDIES:

Discuss the application of one amendment in the Bill of Rights to contemporary life. Cite at least one recent case heard before the Supreme Court. Summarize the arguments of both sides in the court case, and then state your own opinion.

### BIOLOGY:

Discuss one example of symbiosis among plants or animals. Explain how the organisms interact and the benefits and disadvantages of the relationship to each organism.

Sometimes, a teacher will ask you to choose your own topic (related, of course, to what you have been studying)—one that is of particular interest to you. In that case, you will have to come up with a suitable topic and limit it appropriately. On the following pages, you will find several lists of broad, general subjects that may help you think of a topic for a research paper. These lists may be useful when you are searching for a topic for a paper for social studies, science, or an art class. They may also help you choose a topic for a research paper in your English class.

## Inquiry-Based Research

The best kind of research paper starts with a question or questions that truly interest you—questions to which you would very much like to know the answers. Such research is called **inquiry-based**. The research that you do will be satisfying because you are motivated by your curiosity, your desire to find information to answer your very own questions. Here, for example, are several questions that interest the writer of this book. Each could be researched and developed into a paper.

### BIOLOGY:

In some species of birds, the males and females are exactly alike in size, coloring, and marking, while in others the males and females are quite different. Why? What theories have been proposed to explain this fact?

### GOVERNMENT:

What are the arguments for and against English-only laws? Which position do I agree with, and why?

### EARTH SCIENCES:

Why are fossils found in some areas of the United States and not in others?

### ECONOMICS:

After several years of state-run lotteries in (name a state), what conclusions—positive and/or negative—can be reached? In what specific ways do the lotteries benefit (and/or not benefit) the citizens of the state?

## The Writing Process

Your teacher will probably want to approve the limited topic that you chose for your paper. Once your topic is approved, you will follow the same steps (Steps 2–10) as outlined in the text for any type of research paper. The writing process is the same, no matter what the subject. You will need to find or create sources, gather information, organize your findings, and write the first draft. You will also need to allow plenty of time to revise and improve the first draft. If you keep to a timetable and follow the steps in the text, you should be able to turn in a carefully written paper—in any class.

## Three Patterns of Organization

Here are three of the most common patterns of organization for research papers in various content areas:

### COMPARISON/CONTRAST:

When you compare two or more things, you discover and describe their likenesses. When you contrast them, you tell how they are different. You may compare and contrast writers, artists, battles and other historic events, solutions to problems, species of plants and animals—you name it. As long as the two subjects have at least one important feature in common, you can develop a comparison/contrast paper.

### PROBLEM/SOLUTION:

You are most likely to write this type of paper in a social studies class. You identify and describe a specific problem, discuss one or more possible solutions to that problem (or solutions that have actually been tried) and come to some conclusion about the effectiveness of those solutions. In this kind of paper, you will use the critical-thinking skill of evaluation. You will be expressing your own judgments about what does and does not work, and about which is the best and which is the worst solution.

### CAUSE/EFFECT:

This pattern of organization is most likely to be useful in science and social studies. You might write, for example, on some aspect of the environment or on how national and international news (good, bad, and in between) appears to affect the American stock exchanges. You can either analyze an effect (a situation or an event) to find its various causes, or you can start with a cause and write about its effects. Causes and effects are not always clear-cut; they are often a matter of interpretation. This type of paper tends to contain a lot of the writer's own thinking and speculation.

## SOCIAL STUDIES

Social studies covers a broad range of subjects (and classes) having to do with the study of people. All of the following subjects are branches of social studies: history, government, geography, economics, anthropology, archaeology, sociology, and psychology.

# Parts of the Paper

If you are writing for a social studies class, your teacher will probably want you to use the APA style of documentation (see Appendix B). Your paper will have a title page, an abstract (a brief summary of the main ideas covered in the paper), and an introductory paragraph. The body of your paper will be grouped under headings (such as "Methods," "Results," "Data," "Procedure," "Discussion," and "Conclusions") and instead of a Works Cited list (MLA style), at the end of your paper you will have a Reference List.

If you are writing a history paper, your teacher may require that you use one or more **primary sources**. These are documents written during the period you are writing about. The text of the Gettysburg Address is a primary source; so are letters written to President Lincoln and newspaper accounts that appeared at the time of Lincoln's speech at Gettysburg. (A **secondary source** in this case would be a historian's account of the importance of the Gettysburg Address or a literary critic's evaluation of the speech and its structure.) If you are writing a sociology paper, your teacher may ask you to include original primary sources, such as an interview or a survey you create and conduct. Unlike research papers written for English classes, social studies papers often include figures, graphs, and tables. These are referred to in the text and included at the end of the paper.

# Reference Sources

On pages 19–22 you read about general reference sources such as *The Readers' Guide to Periodical Literature*, which indexes some 200 magazines of general interest. The reference sources listed here are specific to social studies. You are likely to find them in a public library or in a local community college or university library.

They may be used for browsing—if you are trying to think of a good topic—or for research in the social studies.

*Africana: The Encyclopedia of the African and African-American Experience.* Kwame Anthony Appiah and Henry Gates, eds. Reading, MA: Perseus Books, 1999.

*Encyclopedia of American History.* 7th ed. Richard B. Morris and Jeffrey B. Morris, eds. New York: HarperCollins, 1996.

*Handbook of North American Indians.* William C. Sturtevant, general ed. Washington, DC: Smithsonian Institution, 1978–1990.

*Life Millennium: The 100 Most Important Events and People of the Past 1000 Years.* Editors of *Life*. Boston: Bulfinch Press, 1998.

*Political Science: A Guide to Reference and Information Sources.* Henry E. York. Englewood, CO: Libraries Unlimited, 1990.

*Women's Studies Encyclopedia.* 3 vols. Westport, CT: Greenwood, 1989–1991.

You may find it easier—and more fun, too—to browse through stacks of recent back issues of magazines, looking for articles that suggest a topic. Try *Ebony*, *Smithsonian*, *American Heritage*, *History Today*, *Psychology Today*, and *National Geographic*. Ask your librarian for help in locating other magazines related to social studies subjects.

## Topic Ideas

The following general topic ideas need to be limited to a specific aspect that you can research with the sources available to you. If you find a general topic that interests you, use the limiting techniques (brainstorming, clustering, questioning) suggested in Step 1 to come up with a workable topic for your research paper.

- One event, invention, or movement that changed human history
- A Native American tribe—its culture, past or present
- Slavery in the Americas
- Racism
- Women's suffrage
- Women's issues today
- A period in history you would like to have lived in, and why
- What you would put in a time capsule
- What education was like in colonial America (or any other period and place)
- Patterns of immigration to the United States in a specific period
- The Great Depression
- The American labor movement
- Child labor in the U.S.; in other countries
- Minimum wage laws
- Juvenile crime/juvenile justice system
- Peer pressure
- Urban problems
- Homelessness
- People with disabilities
- Curfew laws

- English-only laws
- Census data
- Trial by jury
- Freedom of speech
- Guns in American society; in other societies
- Drug education

- Gangs
- Charities
- America's two-party political system
- Voter apathy
- Rights and responsibilities of citizens

## SCIENCE, MATHEMATICS, TECHNOLOGY

In a science class, the term *research paper* may have an altogether different meaning than it does in a social studies class. Instead of a survey of information others have written about a topic, a science research paper is sometimes a detailed report of the writer's original research. This research may take the form of a single experiment or of a series of experiments conducted over a long period of time.

Each year almost two thousand high school seniors submit research papers to the Intel Science Talent Search, a prestigious national competition. These students describe their original research (done under the sponsorship of a teacher and/or scientist) in one of the following categories: behavioral and social sciences, biochemistry, botany, chemistry, computer science, earth and space sciences, engineering, environmental sciences, gerontology, mathematics, medicine and health, microbiology, physics, zoology, and team projects. Judges award more than $300,000 in college scholarships to finalists based on their evaluation of students' use of scientific method, experimental procedures, and detail and accuracy of data presented. For an application and more information about the Intel Science Talent Search, write to Science Service, Inc., 1719 N Street NW, Washington, DC 20036.

You can also write to Science Service, Inc., for a directory of summer programs and internships throughout the United States for high school students interested in science, mathematics, and engineering. (See also www.sciserve.org.)

Find out from your teacher if there are local or state competitions that you can enter. An extremely useful resource for students entering science competitions is *Students and Research: Practical Strategies for Science Classrooms and Competitions* (2nd ed. Cothron, Julia, and Ronald Grese and Richard Rezba. Dubuque, IA: Kendall/Hunt Publishing Co., 1993).

## Parts of a Paper Reporting Original Research

In many respects, the parts of a science paper resemble the parts of a social studies paper. It has a title page and an abstract, which summarizes in a page or less the research project or problem, poses the hypothesis (theory), methods of research, and the results. The introduction includes a brief "review of the literature" (background information necessary to understand your project, including a summary of the most important and/or recent work on the specific topic).

The introduction is followed by a section on the experimental design (sometimes called Methods and Materials) of your project. This needs to be detailed enough so that someone can repeat your study to see if the results are the same. Then comes a section on procedure—what you did, how you did it, how you measured it—followed by a section on your results, including tables of data, charts, and graphs, as well as paragraphs in the text describing your results. Finally, there is a section on your conclusions: the purpose of your experiment, your major findings, whether or not the findings support your hypothesis, possible explanations for your findings. At the end there is a list of works consulted in writing your paper.

## Reference Sources

Here are some reference sources you may use both for browsing—if you are trying to think of a good topic—and for research.

*American Men & Women of Science.* 20th ed. New Providence, NJ: Bowker, 1998–1999.

*Applied Science and Technology Index.* Bronx, NY: Wilson, 1958–1985.

*The CRC Concise Encyclopedia of Mathematics.* Eric W. Weisstein. Boca Raton: CRC Press, 1998.

*Environmental Viewpoints: Selected Essays and Excerpts on Environmental Issues.* Marie Lazzari and Janet Witalec, eds. Detroit: Gale, 1994.

*McGraw-Hill Encyclopedia of Science & Technology: An International Reference Work.* 8th ed. 20 vols. New York: McGraw-Hill, 1997. This encyclopedia is also available in a multimedia edition.

*Van Nostrand's Scientific Encyclopedia.* Douglas M. Considine et al., eds. 8th ed. New York: Wiley, 1997. This encyclopedia is also available in a CD-ROM edition.

If you enjoy leafing through magazines, try recent and back issues of these: *American Scientist*, *Audubon*, *Sierra: The Magazine of the Sierra Club*, *Environment*, *Scientific American*, *Science News*, and *Nature*.

## Topic Ideas

- The single most important invention of the 20th century; what life would be like without it
- Predicting natural disasters
- Do animals feel, think?
- Animal communication
- Animal-rights activists
- Dormant volcanoes
- Preventable deaths
- Endangered environments/species
- Patents/copyrights for scientific discoveries
- Which is more important: nature (genes) or nurture (environment)?
- Benefits of exercise
- Protecting children from accidents and hazards
- Tobacco, alcohol, and other drugs
- Ethical issues in research with human subjects

- Cell biology—latest research
- Math puzzles
- Probability
- Math as a tool
- Catalysts
- Burning of fossil fuels
- Global warming
- Life elsewhere in the universe?
- What's new in the solar system?
- An organism's responses to external stimuli

- Population growth
- DNA
- Gene therapy
- Newly discovered viruses
- Underwater research
- Electric-powered cars
- Acupuncture
- Herbal medicine
- Industrial robots
- Computer software
- Internet issues

## LITERATURE, MUSIC, ART

When you write a research paper for a humanities class (as literature, music, and all the arts are called collectively), you will use the MLA format and the MLA style of documentation. You will follow Steps 1 through 10 of the text.

# Literature, Music, Art Reference Sources

*The American Humanities Index*. Troy, NY: Whitson, 1918–present.

*Benet's Reader's Encyclopedia*. William Rose Benet and Bruce Murphy, eds. 4th ed. New York: HarperCollins, 1996.

*Contemporary Authors*. Detroit: Gale, 1962–present.

*Contemporary Literary Criticism*. Detroit: Gale, 1973–present.

*Dictionary of Literary Biography* (series). Detroit: Gale, 1978–present.

*Encyclopedia of Pop, Rock, and Soul*. Irwin Stambler, ed. New York: St. Martin's, 1990.

*Essay and General Literature Index*. Bronx, NY: Wilson, 1900/33–present.

Gammond, Peter. *The Oxford Companion to Popular Music*. New York: Oxford U P, 1991.

*Gardner's Art Through the Ages*. Richard Tansev et al. Ft. Worth, TX: Harcourt, 1995.

*New Grove Dictionary of Music and Musicians*. Stanley Sadie, ed. 20 vols. New York: Grove Dictionaries, Inc., 1995.

Robertson, Allen, and Donald Hutera. *The Dance Handbook*. Thorndike, ME: G.K. Hall, 1990.

Magazines and journals that may be available in your library include *American Art Journal, American Music, Art & Antiques, Art in America, Architectural Digest, Dance Magazine, The New Yorker*.

## Topic Ideas

- Importance of one artist
- Compare/contrast two artists
- Harlem Renaissance
- Imagists (the movement in American poetry)
- American Romanticism (Realism/Naturalism/Regionalism)— movements in American literature
- Rock and roll
- Reggae (or any other type of music)
- WPA (Works Progress Administration) during the Great Depression

- Analysis and evaluation of a literary work
- Analysis and evaluation of a specific painting, sculpture
- Eastern music
- Persian miniatures
- Folk art/music/dance
- French Impressionists
- Batik (or any other art process)
- Raku (or any other type of pottery)

# Index